Diary of a Human Crow

Hemofiction Novel

by

Juan Trigos

authorHOUSE

□□□□□□□□□□□□□□□□□□□□□□□
□□□□□ □□□□□ □□□□□□□□□□□
□□□□□□□□□□□□□

www.authorhouse.com

First published by AuthorHouse 06/29/04

ISBN: 1-4184-7577-7 (sc)

Printed in the United States of America
Bloomington, Indiana

This book is printed on acid-free paper.

Translated from de Spanish by Daniel Steeger

Cover Design: Luciano Trigos

I

VICEREGAL SPROUTING

Lying down, feeling miserable like a chicken about to be sacrificed. My mother would breed them and as far as I know, they never experienced terror until they saw the knife. I have found feathers on the bed. Black feathers of crows. Also on my wardrobe and on the windowsill.

I am victim about to die. I shall never stop falling into the abyss of parcae, river of souls, abundant and somber. I wish to drown there. I wish that Mr. Death would invite me to join his ship to leave me on hell's side. Time doesn't count; the consciousness has been opened in a brutal way, big. I am able to hear the steps of a canary bird on the windowsill or to look at the pristine chaos, place from where the first amphibious emerged. I know that I have flown. I know that I have bumped into the wall in the back and have fallen in dismay. Feathers on the ground.

Lying down. On a strange bed in the ranch of my cousin Ramon *–go there, buddy, 'cause, get well –He said-. Your vice has gone too far and it's hard to be with you. You immediately loose your instinct and end up walking on the roads of aggressiveness or sadness.*

Night or day. Electric light invades everything: on the roof, lightening softly. Night table lamp, concentrating brightness on the right side of the bed, where supposedly most drunks get well. Canteen memoirs come through of useless discussions. Nauseous, millenniums making bitter throats *–I'm going to throw up (puke)-,* smelly traces of rotten bones and flesh *–I'm going to give birth (be born)-,* It seems as if I were a new person *–modern man, wasted, infinite incoherent, the ties if reason were untied and the boat of deliriousness has weighed anchor, set sail. Since when? Since the world is the world, since time has started to run.*

I know that at times I see through crow's eyes.

Placing myself on the side, on the bed, I see my face in the mirror of the wardrobe. Who am I? Immediate person I am, but also an adventurer posing as prey in the troglodytic era. Hunter in forests and mountains, warrior painted with blood *–me in diverse delirious circumstances-*, today and yesterday get mixed in my language *– shall I never leave this state?* I go from human to crow without pain, smelling of feathers.

I have closed my eyes adopting a fetal position. Open mouth, deteriorated teeth of the present –*my stomach pumps.* Stomachic tremors.

I threw up with guilt. It contained sin: unpunished murder of the girl Teofila, hidden in the depths without depths of my former consciousness. Old consciousness without sovereignty goes adrift, pulsing sweaty dreams, dark nightmares where the sea intervenes and gives life to rancid sensations, dizziness. Vertigo awaits me willing to show what life has, vertigo to be, where we all shall fall –humanity- if our ways are not corrected. Do I dream that I spread open my black wings? I really open them and fly from the bed and back again. Dizziness. Puke.

And I threw person instead. Instead of old bitterness, towards the back wall, painted pale green. Paste of remorse, foreign to what suddenly incarnates into an unknown being.

-Do you know who I am? Do you know whom you have given birth to? –asked the other, the vomit, leaning on the foot of the brass bed. Living presence. Carnivorous locomotion. You know? Why do I want to ignore myself? Why I. Why I –shaking his shoulders some feathers descended to the ground.

-I know that you are you and that I am I, the original. What else do you know about me? Have you seen me fly?

-I don't even know myself. I can't even go beyond the sensation of being in front of you, my father. I can't even inquire myself inside, but I see, I am looking at you, I see that you drink, that you have drunk and feel the thirst. I need to become a brute. I need to enter hell. Have you been there? Any stairs that don't ascend to an alcohol base descends to the worst remorse during a hangover. Down, when I go down, I hear cries of torture –*I cry myself when attacked by the thirst.* That is why I wish to drink. Ignite my shoes and my wings –the man turns into a crow for a few seconds and turns again into a human being.

-I have tequila and rum, what do you prefer? –I offer, pointing at the bottles that are resting on the night table and inside the wardrobe.

Has the man who is throwing up and releasing feathers just appeared? I feel as if we have been repeating his stupid birth over and over again. Come to this world in such conditions... A master out of the nothing. Ordered to be locked away in these four walls. Black viceroy. Mourning viceroy *–damned crow.*

-From what I know, both liquors relax and shake at the same time, brings peace and makes fierce – the vomited viceroy puts in front of himself the liquor bottles, grinning at a fake disgust. I notice that the arm turns into a wing.

-Would you like a beer?

-I would like your experience, what you lived with Teofila –the individual walks in semicircles. From one side of the bed to the other, cup in hand. Why is it so painful to open the mouth and respond? A beak of a crow. Mouth of a person. Black feathers fly.

-Today I see little Teofila as a saint –affirmed, watching the viceroy recover once again his human form.

-What's that of being a saint? –asks the newborn, stopping his march for a few seconds. There it is. There is where the viceroy has been, him, watching me how he asks himself. Tomorrow, if I wake, I shall throw up again and start the same dialog.

-To be a saint is to have died. To have paid for all the sins of the others –I answer after drinking half a glass of beer.

-She fell thanks to your rage- he retakes his nervous motions around my bed. Steps that come and go in an infinite monotony-. I came for a walk to the New Spain, with lack of rage but full of fierceness. I was under the order of Felipe II. Direct in charge. Poor Teofila. You killed her. Isn't it true, Mr. Crow?

-True, she fell thanks to my ignorance –I fly to the wardrobe and from the wardrobe to the bed converted in a crow.

-As I can tell you regret it.

-Not completely. Not in a deep way –I put my beak on my pillow and rub my claws on the white sheets.

-Regret as it should be. Well. Well. Perfect regret. Christian regret. The day I should stop drinking I shall have to… regret. But no. I hear the strong whines that ascend from the stairs of the flee and spread my wings cawing converted in a crow. I shall always fly ascending. Drink and… There was a word that was born with me: Hemofiction –the vomit shows traces of interrogation in the air, smiling with a sarcastic tone at the same time. The mouth turns into a beak during a few hallucinating seconds. I ask myself why do I have to bare his carnal presence. His absolute big presence. The deliriousness, understand, belong to a lighter dimension.

-I was thinking of that word when I threw up: Hemofiction –while pronouncing that word his human head disappeared and instead of it, on his shoulders appeared one of a crow.

-To give birth is not to throw up. You are my father and mother –Now fly to the other end of the room and back. Rest on the footboard of my bed.

-I am the one that I am, wasted. I am the one that I am, drunk –my humanity rests on my bed.

-You try to make clear that another is guilty for what happened.

-Other...no sure whether another...but...something... conspiracy.

-Conspiracy related to the word Hemofiction. –immediately after pronouncing the word with penetrating depth, turns again into a human being. Black viceroy-. I have been involved in many intrigues, you know, as a viceroy...I came to New Spain as a visitor. I blamed several Mexican families with charges of conspiracy. There were many beheaded at la Plaza Mayor. I made larger jails. Filled them with prisoners.

-It seems so, I agree with you as to the word Hemofiction –we kept on looking at each other for a while. Finally he answered, taking his sight off me:

-It's not my intention to agree. I didn't come to the world to agree. I have imposed my willingness to the government many times. I have jumped orders from the king. What if we disagree?

-In what?

-In the meaning of the word.

-We can disagree. It can mean anything to anyone.

-Or with its personal experience.

-Religious Hemofiction.

-Bloody Hemofiction.

-You murdered Teofilita –accused, pointing the index finger and arm stretched at me.

-But I search for redemption –I am crow and so is he.

-Not I. It seems as if I died shortly after going back to Spain. I died while seated, shortly after being reconvened by the king –damned king, false coin. He backstabbed me. Didn't endorse my crimes. He washed his hands. When I went against the opposites. When I cleaned the colony of conspirators. Was I rough? Sure. Tyrant. Yes. But yes. They say that on my shoulder a live crow was found, cawing repeatedly "Hemofiction, Hemofiction". I flew back to the New Spain. For years I have been standing at midnight on the bridge that crosses the ditch behind the school of San Pedro and San Pablo, of the Jesuit priests. The neighbors would hear the word coming out of my beak open with fear, peeling their eyes, without moving from their beds. Hemofiction. Hemofiction –I would repeat every night, making them shake between those who would stay up for my fault. Whilst I say and repeat such hated word, splashes of warm blood through the strikes that I ordered over the sword of innocents and guilty come to my mind, without distinction. Splashes of the irons introduced in the ears and between the teeth to force confessions and accusations. Squirts of blood made rivers that ran and flooded the ditch. Squirts. Force –both flew from the bed to the other end and back.

I gave birth after nine months of pregnancy. Full belly which transformed many memoirs of flesh in motion. There, outside, was the individual thrown out of my mouth. Inquiring eyes. Long legs, straight nose and every other afternoon, beak and wings.

-When did you throw me out?

-Now.

-Today.

-Today and now.

-Yesterday didn't exist.

-Yesterday doesn't exist.

-Tell me about my birth.

I would hear the young voice of Teofila complaining when the disgusts and arches would start *–I shall never be who I was, never, my childhood seems more like a moment belonging now to a prolonged now, expansion of inconsistency, fictitious eternity. I fly from the wardrobe to the bed. Pose my claws on the windowsill and lay my feathers on the pillows. I have contemplated myself in the moon of the wardrobe. Beak and feathers. Open my beak and caw saying* "Hemofiction".

What came from myself in flesh and bone –body of man, maybe like myself- had remained standing very close to the door that entered the room –*human bestiality, visible, vicious, defenseless. The past where the born didn't exist had also remained behind. My unfolded present is the state that covered the past, which really hadn't occurred.*

-I shall not judge you –he proclaimed in a high and energetic voice-. At least not for now. No. I have enough for now with my own dreams dreaming them over and over again. Infamous repetition. Fly to a dark room. There I retake the form of a man's body and punish a wooden Christ. Reason? Because King Felipe II, so special, failed me. Look carefully, he sends me to New Spain with the purpose to stop conspiracy. My voice of order made heads roll. Peace comes. But the intrigue of the audience and of the former viceroy reaches the ears of the king. He sends secret visitors to dispose against my person. I receive the orders and return to Spain. I appear in front of the king almighty and am told off for my conduct. I didn't argue in defense. Nothing. I bit my tongue. Full of anger I sat at home to await my death. And after that, transformed in a crow, I returned to New Spain. I should understand, from the beginning, that I would not be a good governor, as to, a good governor in the eyes of the king, because I was sent to clean with a specific mission. I am not somebody to judge you.

-Then?

-I don't know. I'm outside. Something wants to come out of me. Another viceroy.

-What does a viceroy have to do with me?

-I don't know. I want to give birth to something –imitation.

Not even in my dreams had I sprout my double. I hadn't extracted him from magazine or novel. Nothing. Unedited spontaneity, cawing and flying.

-I am not your double.

-Then?

-I don't know. My stomach hurts. Nauseous.

-Are you going to give birth to yourself?

-It seems so.

-Tell me, what are you thinking of?

-Hemofiction. Crimes at la Plaza Mayor. I let the slayer work. Became friends with him. My buddy. Beheaded hundreds of conspirators. Violent dispossession of their belongings. Torture. Pulled back nails to obtain confession. Yes. Yes. But yes, the punished men yelled. Confess? Yes. Yes. But yes. I did it all for the love of the king. I supposed that I would be rewarded. I was wrong. While I was useful... Damned divine sir, he failed me. Let's say, he used me. I stripped the colony. Nothing would raise under the order for the next forty years at least. Then, the crazy king sent his corrupt missionaries to dispose of me. I was ready to recite my memoirs, the favors I had done for the crown during my governing. I couldn't say anything to him. I swallowed what I wanted to throw up. Guilt, Stupidity, rancor. The divine sir painted himself in white. Condemning me hiding his murderous hand. We're different, you and I, said King Felipe II. Yes, my lord, we are, I answered in silence. I am man of church and you are not. No, I am not a man of church, I responded in silence. After having followed my orders, it is necessary to keep ones position –said King Felipe II and I moved my head in absence. I returned home ready to perish. I prepared my opium pipe and sat to dream on the chair where I was found dead. Overdose? I doubt it. Maybe I ate some of the opium and that was... Now I wake up in four walls, a bit distant. I come and you go, Mister Storyteller. Exchange feathers. I am going to throw up. I feel dizzy. The opium is working.

Now in the body of the other, viceroy born from my interior –turning out just like I –made itself two. Viceroys found. Black and white. Contrast –mass that conforms the specie shall turn delirious.

-Are you drunk? –inquire the two newly born with foolish faces, holding the bars on the footboard of the brass bed.

-A little lack of logic. Lying here, underneath untidy sheets, ignorant of calendars and an alarm clock.

-Do you know what logic is?

-I know that I am an incoherent individual. Ideas slide from me. They come and go in a tangle, especially if I fly from the bed to the back of the room, and from the back of the room...

-Flowers are, I mean, coherent? –both walk around the bed in a same way-. It doesn't seem so and even though...-during an instant of metamorphosis, both viceroys become crows and fly around the room.

-Chlorophyll coherency.

-Coherency of roses and of carnations.

Both have turned into men again.

-Sensitivity of geranium and tangle weed –both make fun of my ingenuity.

-From where does so much plating come from?

-You know.

-You imagine.

-In my imagination flowers belong to the sense of Hemofiction –both viceroys caw, converted in crows, black and white.

-Correct appreciation –affirmed the white viceroy-. I went back to New Spain after cleaning my name to the King and before the Indies Advise. I restored what I could, evil done by myself. It seems as if I died on a chair, after praying my prayers. They say that my right shoulder cawed and albino crow repeating "Hemofiction, Hemofiction". But you'd say that the flowers…

-Correct apparition of the word Hemofiction has blood –the black viceroy made clear-. I see stains on la Plaza Mayor. Stains in the jails of Palacio. Stains in what was my room. Stained clothes. I did it all for you, divine lord. Sir King Lord Felipe II. Praise yourself, on your knees begins the era of terror. Yes. But yes. I made stumps. Yes. But yes. Do you wish to know why I turned into a crow? Why do I caw and repeat the word Hemofiction standing on the handrail at the bridge?

-I don't wish to understand a thing, please, my head hurts, I gave birth to one of you two. I have drunken more. Yesterday I barely smoked a lot of dope. I think that I injected myself, I am not sure.

The viceroy scratches his nose with the point of a feather:

-Searcher for reasons. Professional searcher of causes. Scientific mind. I followed the orders of King Felipe by word. I obeyed. Faced down. I followed to be told off. I was and was the mover of shit. Move shit. I came to move shit. I was useful. So much, that the King qualified me as useless. Goodbye.

-I search for reason and science, yes, because I'm delirious –I say, releasing feathers.

Not precisely. The deliriousness lacks of contents, they only frightened. What's happening to you is more than your natural fear of deliriousness.

-Only I can think the things that happen –be crow and person at the same time.

-What happens to me?

-You entered the dimension of the word Hemofiction –both viceroys caw on the footboard of the brass bed.

We can loose the gain in senses *–I talk in plural because I think humanity exists, like others and I form different parts of human species.* How I wish to hear the screams of the **tamalera** outside the bakery. How I wish to greet the lady at the door. Like walking through a supermarket. Strange human presence. It's a shame that my wife Canuta is far away, feeling down. Far, spilling tears for me, in coherent farewell. Coherent? Why would it be coherent to say farewell to a sick husband? It would all finish if the loose screw would be tightened in its place. That's why a psychiatrist exists, knower of the mind. That's why witchdoctors are here. But I have not gone to visit the curer of souls, of course not, I came to lock myself up in this room. Four unknown walls *–my crow nest. There are feathers on the bed, in and outside my wardrobe, in the bathroom, on the windowsill.*

Science is upside down. Religion involutes towards primitive studies. Turn of the troglodyte or astounding detonation of time. I close my eyes with faith for reality to come back as it was before, when I'd go and come back from work, when I'd enter the canteen smiling, shining with hope. I open them and find myself once again lying on the bed and with the presence of the viceroys. Abysm. I'm going to climb. I have been tangled. My consciousness can't work on its own. I've been burst from the inside. What is inside and what is outside? Human concepts are lost as a crow, my new animal essence.

I'll try not to frighten, but... I'm talking about an unusual complot *–he's to blame that I change shape and get feathers.*

-I don't know anything. Start from the beginning –the viceroys ask, moving their cloaks as if they were wings. To begin is the beginning. The sun warms in heights. Comes the night and then the morning. The maid climbs on the roof and washes clothes. The cook is at the market asking for many kilos of onion and tomatoes. Canuta writes a letter for you, which shall never arrive to your destiny. What did you do? Say it, confess, go ahead, feel yourself at home.

-I planted the crime of Teofila. I planted it in myself. Against my own principles. Knowing that she was innocent. I thought I had a motive... a cause, but now...fly back and forth in the room and rest my legs on the pillow.

-Countryside atmosphere – through the window a draft of air collates which touches the curtains, wardrobe and sheets-. There are farmers that plant vegetal and others, more sophisticated, through into the furrows grains of blood.

-I'm guilty- says my beak.

-No, you're not.

-I killed her.

-By order of whom?

-By order of myself.

-You're wrong.

-I killed in the outside and afterwards threw the seed into my soul.

-Strange concepts to me –says the black viceroy. Soul? Psych? Spirit? The life or energy that allows locomotion to live beings. Our immortal part. As if immortality was a tested quality. As if immortality belonged to somebody. Does it belong to God? Well. Immortal god. But I'm not sure if plants are. I refer to the fact... I refer to the possibility... I want to implicate the possible idea that in reality all flowers are one being. No geraniums and rosebushes. No single gardenias and cloves, but as a whole –due to another draft of wind, three or four twigs full of bugambilia flowers enter the room. I hear thunder.

Water.
Water the crime.
Time went by.
I watered the fertile ground daily like a good farmer waiting for his harvest –thunder gets stronger and the heavy drops start to hit the windows and the roof.
-We are the fruit.
-Black and white.
-But I see you both far from the fact –I see that I am human once again and that I am lying on the brass bed.
-But not to the word Hemofiction –both viceroys caw on top of the wardrobe.

I prayed everyday for what I had planted would be spat out like stinky pus some time. I finally was granted: I expelled the black viceroy and, the black the white one –*three crows and three people.*

Almost simultaneous arching. Vomit had accumulated content for all these year. It had ripened like a Californian apple.

We know that apples change color and consistency. Just like the being I have been carrying inside myself for nine years.

I said to the viceroys, after swallowing a shot of tequila:

-I am part of the delirious universal future and present, part of live history and muddle – today's biographies scrambled with other similar ones from the past-, I am a common person and no mandatary, not even...of course not...political entity, my family is not wealthy –I think of the Habsburgs, of other dynasties, of those who built palaces, czars and ministers, bankers and politicians, priests, those who have become owners of wealth, those who deal, those who plant and distribute.

-You're like us. It seems as if you understand. You'll see, I should search in my mind for the image of the other father like you. You'll see. As time goes on I shall remember the questions asked before I had feathers. I was a child before being a crow. Or not? You understand. Flying is uncomfortable when one is drunk. Danger. I want you to understand why we get feathers.

-I understand- respond, opening the arms as if they were wings.

-I comprehend. Yes. Yes. We had mothers and fathers. Two white and two black fathers. Investment by money. We were spat out to the world in two colors. We transform in white crow and black crow. Young sins. Sins. Drug-addiction. Are we in the power of flowers? We are. I am. You are. We...

-I am not at all like you two –I said to the newly presented, taking a glass of rum from the night table and rushing down two long and sticky sips-. If you're so smart, answer, what is HEMOFICTION?

-Hemofiction? –the viceroys have turned into crows throwing feathers in the air. Now...NOW you look at me posing at the foot of the bed.

-I have been wandering around for a possible meaning of that word for the last fifteen years.

-Fifteen. Six before our conception. Have you been incoherent since then?

-Just like the flowers.

-You shall say then that since then you comprehended the language of the vegetal world. Since then and not before. Before what?

-I have not said such thing. I haven't wanted to implicate it. No.

-Well, we do think so. It seems as if you intuited the disaster. It seems like since then you felt the end. You'll see, it's not that the specie...You'll see...it's not the man...You'll see, if you're the prophet, we...you'll see. Did you hear the explosion? I know that feathers grew on me at the time of death. Is it true that horror has taken over the planet? –Their high voices drill my ears.

I am tempted to look out of the window but I don't dare to. I conserve my fallen position on the bed.

-Supposedly that infamous stream (HEMOFICTION) something like that is occurring, from there comes our double apparition and my necessity to confess what has remained buried nine years in my life –I say with a need to kneel down. True pardon shall turn my fulltime humanity. I shall not turn into crow any more.

-Confess.

-I have never confessed. What is to confess? –Inquires the white viceroy, ignoring my presence-. Supposedly, if you have a white soul…. Supposedly, if you do not sin…Confession?

Catholic action, being myself –superficially-, perfectly atheist. Empty the sack.

-Confess what others have made me do. For example, guide the chambers of torture for the Ampudia family and delight by the screams. For example, grab the whip and use it on Christ Our Lord –*whilst I punish Lord God shall give me feathers.*

-Confess that I am an actor or puppet. Confess. What shall I confess if I have been good and sincere? Yes. We understand.

-Yes. Yes. Confess. I can't confess what I did upon arriving to Mexico. The slayer became my ally. By order of divine Felipe II with must finish off the conspiracy. Yes, yes –said the slayer, behaving in a simple and noble way. We shall hang. Yes, yes –said the slayer as docile as a little bird. We both put the Quijano brothers to drink water. We sat ladies on the hot chair. Slayer and I. The feathered one and the carnal myself. When the slayer turned into a crow, on my shoulder it cawed "hemofiction, hemofiction", I would send my police with terminal orders. Bring so and so or such man accused of supporting the conspiracy against the celestial power of Felipe II.

-What is Hemofiction?-asked the viceroy dressed in black to the viceroy dressed in white –left and right to the being, dark and light presence, equal features and manners in a mirror. The milky mandatary inquires to his dark twin –wing of crow-, thinking of a possible relation that the word could have with blood –tasting of blood the tip of the tongue. Interpellating his other, just the same body proliferating in two –from black came white and the other way round-, like a bacillus in milk, a one-cell being which suddenly multiplies by its polarized bi-participation.

-I like our flavors. I think our ideas. Deliriousness has reached me. It remains materialized in the vatication: "And man shall be dominated by a superior mind".

-But not by us. But not for our empty minds. But not because we lack of logic and memory. But no. But no.

-But yes for the flowers –two branches of Bugambilias hit the crystal of the window.

-But yes. But yes. Irises and Bugambilias –the black viceroy affirms, pointing to the sight where the branches made a noise with a mysterious gesture and deep anxiety, which remains on the surface.

-Evil flowers. I'm talking about evil flowers – I add, in depths to the mystery by underlining with my index finger and with a mark of terror, the place where the branches hit.

-Coke leaves. Opium poppies. Marijuana –the viceroy tries to evade the problem by giving his back to the window. He moves his arms, which turn into wings. Releases feathers.

The bugambilia flowers have disappeared. Honestly, they couldn't have entered because the windows have remained closed. I hear the rain hit the windows.

-I don't remember any explosion. Yes, the world is coming to an end… Silence. Quiet bomb. In exchange I do remember seeing pigs arrive to the ranch. Chicken scratching to get maggots and worms. That and a crow waiting for me in the bathroom, claws on the lavatory.

-To what world and what does the end mean to a drinker? Neither terms nor catastrophes, it is necessary to show oneself as a positive being –the white viceroy perorates riding on the thigh of his equal-. As far as I know, the final orders of the king were revoked before reaching the port of Veracruz. As far as I know, it wasn't I who had so many noblemen killed, especially all conspiring natives. But I dreamt of… what did I dream? Oh, I dreamt that I came descending, flying over stone steps that would lead to immense chambers of torture. A nightmare. Why did those men and women chained to the wall moan? I lifted my torch and looked over the wall to a bleeding Christ because he had just been hit –with the fist, whip, nails. I reached to Him in the dream. I asked him: But Mr. Jesus, who has hit you. You, responded the Christ in a rude manner and I flew back the stone staircase of the nightmare until I woke up in a jump on the chair where I had died. But I did not wake up as a man, but as a crow. I wanted to cry for help and cawed: "Hemofiction, Hemofiction".

Both viceroys came out themselves at importunate moments, points of immense anxiety and wishes to flee *–fly, flee to the responsibilities.* They had exited, time past, consumed fact, throwing feathers in the air. I wasn't that sure of haven given birth to the black viceroy. But the mind had registered the moment of emergency. I had thrown him up. I had opened my mouth and... thrown the mature and dark son *–same one that flies in the room. Back and forth from wall to wall. Poses on the lamp and on the wardrobe. Sips **cubas** with its beak and then flies clumsily and the human crow crashes against everything around us.*

-Life is over with me –I babble with rage-, I suppose they have not come to persuade me not to commit suicide –and feel the gun that I keep in the draw of my night table.

-No. You can shoot yourself or throw yourself from the roof. No. We are apart. You live, we live. You are, we are and the crows, too. Tomorrow we shall go to the market to buy meat and vegetables. Tomorrow we shall drive in the crow's claws over the bridge as it hits midnight. The neighbors shall hear our macabre cawing repeating "Hemofiction, Hemofiction". They'll dream of bells highlighting the mystery. BongBong. Some innocent creatures shall interrogate their parents about the sense that possess the word and the adults, as usual, shall slide from the tangent saying: Tomorrow you'll have to wake up early, go to sleep, tomorrow is another day.

-Did you ever give a dozen roses to your girlfriend Teofila? -asked the viceroy sweetening the tone, shining his romantic eyes.

-Red roses in her heart. Dripping roses -the black viceroy made fun of him.

-Shining petals showing my way out of paradise, my departure from Eden. I have chewed on forbidden fruit *-that is why I have turned into a crow, which is why I caw at nights, which is why I fly wall to wall in my room.*

Teofila stopped breathing. Suspended heartbeats. Suspended.

-She suddenly became dead, thanks to me -I put ice in the glass and half fill it with white rum. I add Coca Cola and taste it.

-Thanks to your evil flowers. You're not to blame. Neither are we -the march of the viceroys has been suspended. They look and act as if mirrors were in front of each other. Metamorphosis. Now, like crows, they fly and pose on top of the wardrobe.

-Since then, I want to understand, the logic...

-Yes, the logic...

-The logic...

-From what I know...man...

-What man?

-We. The human race, divided in masculine and feminine.

-Black and white, like us. White galaxies and black galaxies. Light planets and dark planets. Did you eat peyote?

-The crows fly into the bathroom and leave shortly, to reseat after a while on top of the wardrobe.

-Pure alcohol.

-You don't know how to grease words nor phrases -the criticism of the black viceroy, black crow, hurts me. With resentfulness I take a sip of my **cuba libre** and respond with contained anger:

-Well, I knew how to do it. I used to do it at home.

-What home?

-Where my wife awaits me. Home.

-I imagine dining room and living room. I imagine bath and kitchen. Home -the black viceroy, suddenly humanized and

28

standing in front of the headboard of the bed, swinging his index finger around his head pointing out of madness. I see that feathers are falling.

-I live in a house. I am now here, in this room of my cousin Ramon's ranch because I came to rest.

-Alcoholic repose.

-Before coming here, you mean, before the world... You had a house or... you lived in it. And what if your wife played a joke on you and introduced you to the madhouse?

-Do you know something about the exterior?

-Nothing. Absolutely nothing –listening to the rattling of leaves stuck to the crystals of the window.

-But it exists. It at least existed. Just like the madhouse. Place where the ill minded rested. Incoherent beings like you. He and I existed. You and us. Two viceroys and two crows. Three and three.

-Depends on what we comprehend as existed –I say lying down, incapable of taking a look and proving that the rest of the ranch remains there.

-You can touch the exterior –the white viceroy rubs the brass sphere that crowns the footboard of the brass bed.

-You could touch it if you left. Although, of course... touch...touch is no guarantee. We have touched walls, these walls. We haven't touched ourselves.

I don't dare to move. I remain lying on the bed. I light a cigarette. Contemplate my hands. Move my fingers. I am human. Now I am. Tomorrow... I stick my eyes to the pillows and see black feathers.

Launch platform to the absurd. Inside the whole new dimension the coherent has lost use.

In infinite occasions I feared to acquire suddenly the vision of flies and bees, listen to the stars through the exquisite ear of birds and bats.

I tell you, with the fingers on my chest:

-I am the body, and you're not. Individual existence. Individual thought. I take decisions. God hasn't sent you. Neither has the devil.

-Nobody has brought us here —both mumble, moving again around the bed, as if the last affirmations may have unblocked the mechanism that maintained them mirrored in front of each other.

-My past.

-Yes, your past.

-I may have thought it once, maybe. I may have dreamt it. As a child.

-Never, on the contrary, you may have conceived to leave the mental tumor turning it into putrid matter. See tumor as the crime. Because you killed. Because you murdered Teofila. Innocent little Teofila.

-Keep the words, I'm dizzy.

-We shall take you to the disheveled sense.

-And if I don't wish to go?

-We shall take you anyway.

-Am I supposed to confess my crime before you?

-You can do it, but it won't help.

-May I have lost my ear?

-You are listening to us.

-But inside the vortex- they fly and pose on the wardrobe. They fly and pose on the footboard of my bed.

I suddenly found myself immersed in the chaos, broken the strings of the false structure that still sustained me.

-Have I died through intoxication?

-You're alive. You exist. We exist. We move. We've been born. We feel necessities. In a short while we shall pass to the lavatory.

-Why do you ask or wish to disembowel the word Hemofiction?

-Because it's not a word.

-What is it then?

-A word with veins. Word with a thick jungle of veins. Blue veins. Veins full of spiritual blood. Veins that pump inside of our beings.

-I already said that I killed Teofila, now... now... please...

-We don't know no Teofila.

-She was my girlfriend.

-Human concept. Roses simply fall in love.

-I was in love in a simple way.

-But you talk of a couple. But you suggest the vague idea of aspiring to matrimony and happiness.

-I aspired to that, yes, and spoilt it all.

-You say that you remain married.

-That's right.

-You say that your wife loves you.

-That's right.

-But your wife is called Canuta and not Teofila.

We know that birds sing. We know that the sun rises and sets, spreading nostalgic shine.

-Who knows such things? Where does the sun come from? Where is it going? – The black viceroys stares towards the soffit-. Are you affirming that the sun moves? That the enormous mass of light walks in the firmament?

-Since I was a child I knew...

-Another concept, childhood... you are surrounded with shells of thought. You'll see. You entered here; you gave me birth, black viceroy and crow. You and I started to live of drinks. And later was my equal white granted. My contrary and not my same. Albino crow. Identical in extreme. Identical in shape, but... Now you come up with the pilgrim idea of keeping away. Touch.

-As I can see, we shall probably never leave this room. I shall keep flying in this room.

-Not even by flying could we leave –the black viceroy affirms going back and forth from the bed to the back of the room, shaking his black wings.

Let's suppose that the universe hides itself in the sense of the word Hemofiction. Where? In the sub-world of the insects?

-I've died, haven't I?

-To a certain degree. Yes, in a certain way. Yes, as to your latest consciousness... We could assure... But there's no appetite that assures but drinking. Could you prepare yourself another drink?

Man is king of creation –was. That's what it looks like –seems. That's how we want to believe.

I serve **cubas** to the viceroys-crow. The three of us listen with exaggerated cautiousness to the sounds: cracking of ice and the flow of rum and coke. Outside is dominated by the silence. Strange tickling of the **bugambilias** branches on the windows.

-King of creation. The phrase sounds odd. King. Creation. We don't comprehend truly to the truth what it... Are you trying to say something? Are you trying to mean something? –The black viceroy draws question marks in the air.

-Confusion. The concepts have been swept away from me. I'm drunk. It seems so.

-Not that much. Just a little drunk –the white viceroy corrects me overacting, allowing honey to drip off his gestures and tone of voice.

-You talk about an equal world, slightly changeable.

-The one I know.

-The one you knew, perhaps.

It has become night –Why have I suddenly felt the day passing if before…? Intense rays of the moon penetrate through the crystals of the window –silvery shines reflect on the capes of the viceroys-crow. I dare not to stand up and prove that there is nothing else beyond these four walls.

-I do believe so. Yes. But yes. I think that he has lived outside of this room –assures the white viceroy with a mellifluent tone-. I love to dream that things remain where they are, that the sun rises every morning, that I wake up next to my wife that loves me, that she serves me breakfast… that I go to work after receiving a loud kiss at the door. That my dreams lack of white wings –now the albino crow caws on top of the wardrobe.

-Zero stability –assures black viceroy kicking the feet of the bed. His fingers melt into claws. He has turned into a crow and caws on the footboard of the bed "Hemofiction, Hemofiction". The other viceroy also repeats "Hemofiction, Hemofiction". Two founded crows, black and white, fix an evil stare at me. I close the eyes. Open them. Once again the viceroys look at each other in the mirror. Zero balance –remarks the black viceroy, ignoring his transformation.

Nevertheless… We see the milkman who whistles upon delivery and we sigh of relief: another day that nothing occurs, another day that the monstrous fence gives us a sensation of stability. Nevertheless… We see the gas truck and the garbage truck. Clerks walk by on their way to work swinging their belongings.

-Nothing is really happening. Nothing –the white viceroy maintains shaking his head, without making the atmosphere of a catastrophic sensation disappear.

-You are before me. There. Existing.

-So?

-A moment ago you weren't.

-So?

My mind could be similar to the universal peace –I think, exist. What I see has always been the same. I am relaxed. Very. For this reason, I shall stop drinking. Why should one drink if you know that the door of the house remains in its place, just like the lock? I have not left feathers on my bed. My dreams have been pleasant. I look at myself in the mirror on the wardrobe and say to myself "all is the same".

-What you have seen has always been the same. Garbage truck full of garbage men and garbage. Milk truck full of milk and milkmen. So much knowledge. So much tranquility. Dawns and falls. So much tranquility. You have called us, for example, doubles. Your doubles? Are we you and ourselves? Doubles of the crow or doubles of the person?

-You seem to talk superficially.

-I insist, you called us doubles.

-I was wrong, excuse me.

My brain has materialized for the viceroys, the same ones which observed me with a clear curiosity –What kind of tranquility can run in a uncontainable creator?

-Tranquility. We don't know what it means what you suppose that God understands. We are chatting, but you don't wish friendliness because you immediately introduce foreign concepts. Let's start from the present, please. Immediately, please. From right now, please.

-Night and day. Time. Hell. Four or five weeks form a month. Twelve months a year –I say in an insisting tone, hypnotic.

-You feel like talking. You feel like confusing. Yesterday… yesterday could have been how you suppose. But that was yesterday, because today… -both viceroys reach metamorphosis and fly around the room.

Night falls and we go to have diner –all other existing beings think as I do. Tablecloth, cutlery, glasses, and napkins.

-What existing beings?

They think that they are not threatened –live beings in danger. I suppose the contrary. We are. Of death. I have fallen into the divine curse.

-You talk about before the end. You talk about before. Before is not now. Damn it. Why do we have to talk about before if now exists?

They, my equals –men, women, children-, they have dinner in similar to mine. They pray in similar churches. The rest of the beings have invented me or I have invented them. We have worked together. We have gone to vote.

-What are you talking about? Is there something beyond these four walls? –The beak of the albino crow caws saying "Hemofiction, Hemofiction".

Today I am, but tomorrow... Die is to dissolve, enter the nothing *–perhaps the consciousness of the crow. Crow myself. Dehumanize. To get lost in the animal unconsciousness.*

From this concept where everything is right and seems logical, we enter the emptiness. I contradict myself. Meaning, facts contradict me. Have I died?

The Romans which ate opium or breathed in marijuana smoke in the century II were erased from historic and transpersonal memory. Some, very few, are conserved in a way that seem too precarious between the pages of history.

-What history? Some. Nobody. The two words come to say the same. What comes from your thought and what remains... Perfect similarity. There is nothing beyond o closer to your own head. Well, it's us two. Black and white. Crow and man. Nothing.

-Apart from you two. Apart from what I remember of what once was. Apart from what I remember what I once was. Two. It's you two. One came out of me, and the other...

-Two or one seen from different found angles.

-We're supposedly descendents of Adam and Eve.

-Yes, supposedly.

It shook Eden. We ate from the evil tree –ecstasy. And we all turned into crows. I see feathers on the bed and on the floor. Black and white.

Untranscendental. Safe and marvelous monotony. The sun rises. The sun sets –*I fly from my bed to the back of the room and turn to pose my claws on the pillows.*

-I bathe, you… I pee, you…

-Both of us have for breakfast bacon or chorizo and eggs.

-Have you ever loved your wife?

-Sure, once.

-More than Teofila?

-Teofila was. My wife is. I came to rest. Outside awaits the world that I knew. Outside… Let's go to restaurants and to work –an apparent similarity, which is liked from comics and magazines, which enters the dance halls and is heard by the same type of music.

-You can put music on if you want to.

Nothing is like thinking or…the other way round. Men dream of our importance –without differences, everyday we're closer to the ants.

-Music sounds. It's an influence to the flowers.

-Strengthens the floral thought.

-Trees like music.

-We're talking about the exterior. Outside there are trees and bushes.

We're talking about outside, about the flowers.

-Floral exterior that dominates the interior of the storyteller.

I'd call myself ephemeral science. Religion... At school I learned to sum. They asked me to honor the flag. Shortly before getting rid of Teofila –just a few years- The morality teacher had given me a star out of good conduct and stuck it on my forehead.

-Ignorance. That person knew that you would attack your girlfriend –the black viceroy moves towards the sound machine but stops right before putting it on.

-If she had known, she wouldn't have given me a star. The teachers, in the exterior world, are descent people, they were, some of them, before the flowers...

-But the teacher had no way to know about your interior. But no. In exchange the flowers in your garden knew. The trees on your street.

-The teacher never supposed that you'd smoke pot.

-Never.

-She never supposed that you would lose yourself drinking.

-Never –finally the black viceroy presses the on button and a bolero starts to play. I start to fly around the room, releasing feathers.

-If you want to be someone –my mother used to say- Stay away from drugs. Don't drink. Don't smoke. Don't even think of pinching yourself. The morphine-addicts complain about pains, lose interest, just like alcoholics and potheads *–they end up turning into animals, crows.*

-Interest in what? –the black viceroy presses the button to turn off the radio.

-In life.

-In what men call life.

-Precisely.

-Mom suggested:

Pay attention whether the interlocutor has dilated and shiny pupils. Does he have mood swings or suffer of euphoria followed immediately by depression. Dad injected himself once, you know. Dad would hide in the lavatory, I mean, in the bathroom. He'd never put his sleeves up. I took his vice away, you know... you know... Your granddad would throw up the intelligence of your father, because he never thought that he would get on with his life. Who ever enters the darkness of syringes...

Before seeking refugee in the room of the ranch, how many times did I greet my boss at the office? Good morning. Let's say, nothing has happened yet –good afternoon, let's say, the sun went up and the planet never burst. Markets are still selling pumpkins and oranges and gas trucks are still with men knocking to fill up tanks, and the postman rings the doorbell and the maid goes out to sweep the path and wash the cars.

Catastrophic predictions seem ridiculous to an atmosphere full of harmony and invulnerability –what threatens mankind? Nothing. Bombs. Nothing. Burglary. Nothing. Superiority deliriousness. The reader shall understand –If my writings reach your eyes- there shall be hard feelings through my words.

Whilst I thought that man –humanity- was pampered, I saw God as our ally –today I suppose that he's a buddy of plants and flowers.

I'm thinking of hemp and opium poppy –Symbol of the goddess of fertility Demeter -, henbane, belladonna, and mandrake. I'm thinking of opium's popularity. Aesculapio used it in his temples, offered to his patients for "healing daydreams". Heraclides of Tarento, Doctor of Filipo, father of Alexander Magno, pledged to use and diffuse it. Galeno also used poppy juice to calm any type of pain. Opium. Symbol of Dioniso –God-Plant. Mass. Dioniso dissolves –curiously- The personal identity and invites its believers to participate in the orgiastic community *–suddenly I discover, I am conscious, that I think of flying around the room.*

Where are we going? Where there's no return. To the possible and impossible infinity.

But you still believe –you go towards God, I say. But you still think of kneeling in front of Jesus. But you still think there shall be salvation. I don't believe it anymore –not in this human god, maybe in this God-Plant. It has changed with all the rest –the Christian church did well on opposing the faith in hallucinating trips, pleasure trips, fleeing trips, offered by infinite substances like mescaline, cocaine, lysergic acid, marijuana, hash. Saint Augustine rejects any curious insane science, the French king Childerico condemns the use of diabolical plants. Charlemagne calls opium works of Satan.

While he shaved, my father would say: Tomorrow is another day –he'd sigh with relief and nostalgia, he had gotten free from the syringes.

-How many times did he inject himself morphine? –the black viceroy stopped playing the mirror game with his equal.

-I don't know, nobody knew.

-Your mother knew.

-Half.

-She sighed for another reality.

-So much she turned delirious.

-I don't know. I don't know.

There was trust before. Nobody dared to think that we were in danger –despite the assault and kidnapping crime wave. Too deep horrors –the evil ignores whether they have been possessed. They'll know when they are turned into a stem or stalk, when they get petals of eyes and ears.

-Immediately after turning human, the black viceroy says:

-I'd like –a lot, by God –to grow in a pot turned into a geranium, azalea or a marijuana flower. Then, into evil... maybe I'd enjoy the green metamorphosis. Contradiction: Stems don't drug themselves, flowers don't kill each other, but... But they do kill humans and crave for power. But yes. But yes. The duties of the flowers started from the lowest grade of consciousness... The weak... The foolish... The crazy that wanted to become rich... were absorbed, taken, and poisoned. Although, I do like to think of the pot, grow there; beatify the empty space there, receiving air. I shall be cut and be smoked by somebody. Crazy young people shall make cigarettes out of my leaves.

-As to me, along a sidewall, like a net I'd like to grow, green and fresh –responded the white viceroy-. We were talking about power. Green domination. Unmeasured ambition. We were talking about the exterior: sun, rain, buildings, houses, avenues, and cars. We were implicating open air-pollution. We were supposing or imagining children going to school in white-painted school buses. I dream of good teachers inviting their pupils to pray –the white viceroy sighs deeply and flies to the window.

-The books will be lost. History of mankind will be lost –assures the black viceroy.

-We're lost, I understand that. We shall not find each other anymore.

On the contrary, we shall find each other. The miracle of life finds itself just around the corner –I assure with sarcasm, followed by a slurp from two good sips.

-Well. You continue supposing that there are corners and turns, churches and markets, denied wives and teachers, vocational doctors.

-Vocational doctors? Only between humans can vocational doctors grow and breed, the eyes of the white viceroy-crow glow a romantic shimmer.

-What have you eaten, love, what has made you so upset? —my wife Canuta had asked, cursing the sub repetitive ingestion of drugs, just before the heat of the crisis which had taken me to the ranch where the viceroys had appeared and the crow wings —consider the parental addiction. Damned inheritance. Son imitates the father.

-I do not eat, love, I drink. I enjoy distilled grapes and sugar-cane with equal pleasure. Out of malt spill delicious brands of beer, and from blue **Agave** airy tequilas. Do you believe that the ingestion is turning me crazy?

-Drinks are drugs- she affirms, coming closer to me, in the bed.

-A cheap way to not stay in the same place. They assault my dreams by gallop, winged nightmares —I respond, touching her nipples with my fingertips.

-If you need to take a trip, go and rest at the ranch of your cousin Ramon. Believe in God. Believe in me. What changes your mood is hazardous. During Medieval times and the Renaissance alcohol consumption grew in fearful ways. In some monasteries, Dioniso was praised, God-Plant, by singing Catulli carmina and Carmina burana. We are lost. Consumption and production is

growing. Paracelso —proselyte doctor- deepened our disgrace by defending opium. The patients —who were really addicts- would follow him, always in need. And talking about opium, also a doctor named Thomas Sydenham contributed to our actual ruin creating laudanum, which carries his name. Recipe: opium is watered down with wine from Malaga, saffron, cinnamon powder and clove. Cromwell, King Charles II, Louis XIV and Richelieu were addicts, just like many more. We must stop if we wish to…

My wife covers her face to cry.

-But we don't want to stop, love —I say licking her tears.

-To stop would mean depression —welcoming. You shall be sad for a time and… after…

-War between drug lords. War between countries. Stop? How?

-Francisco I of France would cut the ears off of drunken people. I would get tired of strangling Chinese and Mexican drug dealers, American, Bolivian and Colombian. In central squares, major squares, were allowed, between other things, to punish all those who would deviate from the paths of consciousness, the paths of humanity as a specie –my wife kisses me on the lips.

-The true specie… -caressing her shoulders.

-Man has believed.

-It's not true. The mind of man.

-Inferior mind.

-Addict mind.

-Addictive.

-Dominated mind.

-Our privileged site is envied by many created beings, between others some poisonous plants –then I didn't catch clearly what was implicated by my wife. Poisonous jealous plants?

I say with enthusiasm, convinced that I'll kick my addiction whenever I feel like:

I shall take the next train. Take the next truck. Get on the first bus. I must lie down soon at the closest distance. You'll see, I shall miss you.

-I hope so.

-I shall dream with you. I shall kiss your thighs and bellybutton.

-What else annoys you?

-Alcohol. Work. Alcohol. Work –and what I'm about to tell you, Canuta. I shall face it at the loneliness of the ranch. What supposed my bad deed. I wanted to fall on my knees and cry. I wanted to go to the old church and hold a long and commotional conversation with some good friar. Bad deed. Sin. Act that will take me to hell –now I know: invisible thought traveled to my brain and ordered the death of Teofila. It talked about traveling, but I am not sure. To travel implicates time, motion in space. The planted thought appeared, surged, grew in my interior giving an immediate foot to an evil act. Such thought and such act didn't emerge from original humanity. For a moment chlorophyll ran through my veins.

Green poison. My stone heart got covered by clovers. I killed. Act condemned by the catholic church.

I denied giving reason to my wife. I shall keep quiet what I was already living, dressed and sitting on the brass bed, in a room lent for an impossible rest. External polarization of my vice royal being. Two in one. Three in one. We were able to stay together during many years, but... at the end... explosion. Unusual that it didn't happen at home, watching TV next to Canuta or at the office. If it had happened so, I would have had to blame the alcohol –and the drugs- the apparition of the viceroys-crows found –but to blame the alcohol meant to drop it and I wanted to keep on getting drunk –*continue*, roots to the complot of the plants and flowers.

-Who gets hooked, difficultly... -she holds the cry, was saying goodbye from my mind showing infinite tenderness.

-Fishing takes place with two baits: money and pleasure. I know. Now I know. I shall try to... Promise, Canuta. I shall not let the hidden purpose of the flowers...

It's about getting on through the freewill of the person, submit –that's what flowers want. Addictive essence. Infinite soldiers that spread in all nations.

-The same humans turned into agents for the flowers. Degraded humans –I say just to say, keeping the string.

-The same humans, weak, feed the complot. Darkened soldiers. Grey entities, idiots and idiotic –she hugs me.

-You'll see, my dear –I said to Canuta-, you're right, the one who drinks too much, ends up seeing angels that turn into demons. The one that ingests drugs, ends up murdered. I shall get cured at the ranch of my cousin, you'll see.

I want to specify here that the visions of my alcoholic deliriousness are of persecutory character. The viceroys harassed me – from the depths with no bottom of my unconsciousness –because they wanted to find out, this has become their function since they became present. Know the reason of my deliriousness.

-You're mistaken. Not at all –they respond without turning around to face me.

I asked:

You suppose, viceroys, gentlemen, that flowers are breaking the consciousness of time.

-Flowers are helped by an infinite number of agents that look human –assured the black viceroy without looking at me, keen on the mirror game with his equal-. Bodies of people imbued to the millenary vengeance of certain evil flowers that have ambition for power.

-Drug dealers. Producers. Politicians.

-And consumers. For millenniums have their weak consciousnesses taken over and serve or impulse the domination of the specie –the viceroys, turned into crows, caw on top of the wardrobe: "Hemofiction, Hemofiction".

I found myself immersed in live situation –the crows exist, lizards, horses and people of similar ways –I repeated to convince myself.

-We live, yes. But outside…. You suppose that there are animals. We are rational animals. Being with beliefs of superiority. Created with similarity to God –they transform into crows and turn into human forms within seconds, without pain.

I don't want the reader to feel wrong sensations: the closeness of the viceroys didn't make me nervous as to being with some dangerous animal, serpent or scorpion. I talk about an intense life –closeness to dream and madness.

-If somebody is crazy here… We cannot forget that we were born and brought up here in the stomach of an addict –the viceroys drink to the mirror.

-If somebody needs a psychiatrist… We must not forget that the anxiety that was planted here by the flowers was inherited.

-But yes, of course, you were right: we live with intensity – both let out a huge laugh and immediately start cawing "Hemofiction, Hemofiction".

-That is, intensity. Intensity. Strong presence.

As much as the used space wishes to transform itself, so does time.

-Let's start from the beginning, my storytelling friend.

-Let's start from now and not from yesterday.

-Yesterday or the day before yesterday you killed Teofila.

-Yesterday or the day before yesterday you talked with your wife Canuta.

-Yesterday or the day before yesterday she suggested you to go to the ranch. Let's suppose with trust and credibility your imaginary past. Lets think that maybe… beyond your deliriousness…

Nobody will deny that in altered states of consciousness –ecstasy, delirium- come similar hallucinations.

-Similar or unedited. Similar if the truth outside is a concrete fact. Unedited if you are the delirious cousin. Let's call the first true contagious one. The first one lost in the floral immensity convenient for the flowers. As a child did you see things? If you existed then, in your past, I would have said two things: either you're a saint or you need a treatment based on drugs.

The viceroys wander about in the room thinking.

I'm no saint and I didn't find myself then –and even less now –under psychiatric treatment based on drugs –another way to succumb the domination of evil flowers.

-Suppositions. As a child, I talk about your birth… Were you born? Was there really a baby, Mr. Storyteller? For us, it's fine, you can submerge in old memories, of course.

-The pre-birth descents were not familiar to me. Neither were the transpersonal transports. I am a murderer –that's what I thought-, no shaman.

-You were a visionary child? Child?

-Visionary child who hides with alcohol? –The viceroys once again walk around the bed. Moonlight rays fill the room. It is night. Time to go to sleep. But I can't sleep. Neither can the viceroys-crows.

I have never had a vision like North American Indians do –I think about Crazy Horse and Sat Bull. I haven't eaten peyote either. The viceroys flourished of diverse nature, to know: the necessity to warn mankind –face to face and through my writings –about the conspiracy of plants and flowers.

-Do you know anything about that conspiracy? –the black viceroy asks, spitting. Neither do I. If I don't know about something, what can I warn about?

-I don't know anything about kinky business. Nothing. I'm an optimist. Open or… shall open my eyes tomorrow to tomorrow thinking about the Holy Spirit, in the universal conversion to Christian belief –asseverate the white viceroy, in sadness.

-The man, our father or twin or delirious creator talks about warning. And I say that that can be told. Warning. As a matter of fact, we have been warned many times before.

But to warn is not to save. It was told that Jesus Christ warned and marked the way. We all- do exist, including the viceroys-crows-, we are unable to control our own structural formations unable to use the wand of virtue, witch and black magic style. My salvation –and that of the world shall come, maybe, from the compensation of the word or concept HEMOFICTION.

-Hemofiction, Hemofiction –the white and black crows caw on the footboard of my bed as the sun starts to rise. A few rays of light illuminate suddenly my actual situation.

-What does HEMOFICTION mean?

-I don't know what HEMOFICTION is –I affirm from my bed, letting some smoke out of my mouth –first morning cigarette. They didn't attend me, they continued in their own and early born existence –they lacked of spirit to be prophets, warmth to be leaders or directors.

-Vocabulary and confusion is growing. You should really take charge of messing up what already is messed up, dear storyteller.

With time –I thought-, these viceroys who came from my pain shall enlighten new ideas, privileged concepts that collocate my intelligence on a superior stage of development –far from drugs and contagious evilness to the infinity of non-smart men.

-I expect to be told off. I expect to be spanked. Your wife, in reality your mother Canuta, shall pick up from the ranch a redone child, spiritually speaking. It is not so. If you should be interested sending messages to mankind, we'd rather leave you flying in the vortex of deliriousness. Example to the non-existent exterior. Catholic example. Puritan example. Unhappy ending.

-Will then my end be unhappy?

-One and then another final. Finals.

-Many and other finals. Don't you understand that nothing finishes in the stories of the galaxies?

-What do the galaxies have to do with me? I talk about death or… about end, ending on the streets, it is said, ending up hanged, it is said, ending being the unhappiest of the mortals, poor and crazy, it is said.

-That can happen, of course it can –affirmed the black viceroy without looking at me, marching the other way of his equal around my bed.

-But also the contrary. Precisely, a happy ending. I like them –the white crow is lying on the pillow and releases two tears.

The door has been opened. Through her, vegetal ambition has gotten through. If some day Martians should arrive on earth, they'll know about our disastrous extinction. The reader shall judge after reading these notes what happens in the interior –I wish to clarify the betrayal of the specie.

-Now I do think that you're drunk, Mr. Storyteller. Lost.

-Now a do believe you need to enter the madhouse.

-The psychiatrists shall say that you suffer of paranoia.

-Persecution deliriousness.

-But you were saying something about HEMOFICTION.

Yes. I was saying... Am I talking about spiritual alchemy? I'm not sure. My changes can result too intimate and personal –also my deviations. Too local, a say. Most men –today- think that we are all the same specie –consider human those who allow the vegetal complot. What am I if I transform myself into a crow and back to my human form over and over throwing black feathers?

-Sooner or later chlorophyll shall start to circulate in our veins instead of blood–the black viceroy comments, lighting a cigarette at the same time as myself. The viceroy-crow puts on the electric light.

-I do believe that man is man. Crow and man. Two doubles I mean, humanity is one and not two or a thousand, just like the flowers. One flower. We have eyes and hands. We have a similar appetite although we may eat different things. For example the Spanish and their **fabada**... For example Italians and their pasta. I prefer to keep a diet, eat healthy, not spicy nor greasy. That is why... not that... it means o signifies that I consider myself different to most humans, although I... meaning, I take care and be.... Good... .although some day.... Plants lack of diets.

-Abstract equality- the black viceroy comments-. Plants with no teeth and humans toothed.

-What do you mean? Explain. I know there are silly people and smart people. I know there are some that are cultured and ignorant. Vegetarians and meat eaters. Delinquents and respectful people to the law. Who don't respect the law... well... lack of human consciousness, and if that occurs...well, well... someday, maybe tomorrow, if we still exist, chlorophyll shall be running through our veins instead of blood.

Equality between humans and humanoids influenced by the vegetal consciousness? –that's what I thought before I saw the viceroy emerge right in front of my eyes –warning. Ultimatum.

-I keep on thinking the same. Whites, yellows, dark… equality. We are all children of dear little God –affirms the white viceroy, accelerating his march around my bed.

-I, in exchange, think of ducks and lizards, differences so big as to the tail –the black viceroy pronounces, pushing down a drink of rum.

-Only one humanity, one. Like flowers are… many and diverse but in the end… One floral consciousness. One.

That's what I thought. But I had stopped to believe in it. I could be me and at the same time a floral agent. I hadn't chewed on opium without a reason. I hadn't smoked marijuana without a reason. I hadn't ingested rum without a reason. Silly I. Poor me. I was falling on the slide towards vegetal unconsciousness, towards hell, towards the vortex.

-If man –the true one- manages to undo themselves from the influence of plants and flowers, they could become super-man –the black viceroy says, throwing smoke at the same time as I do-. Goodbye to fleeing and the way of spirituality. Ascending straight towards the sky. But no. But no. That… that is impossible of all impossible things. While man is man, they will keep on being man; they'll never get to be to the same scale of a super-man… I mean, while there are men on earth, drug shall rule over all infant consciousnesses.

Electric light has become dull.

-Of course that we shall get to sit on the thrown of the super-man. On the contrary the specie shall pick up chlorophyll. We shall lose eyes and tongue.

-We shall lose locomotion. Instead of feet, roots.

-We shall release pollen instead of semen through the genders.

The Nietzsche super-man wanted to prove itself in an unfamiliar and provincial chamber? Of course not. Delirious. I touch it. Without pain I turn from crow to human and from human to crow just like in dreams.

-Let's not forget the philosopher, Nietzsche, he liked opium. He was crazy and an opium addict.

-Let's not forget that he had the intuition of individuality being a possible exit.

-Daisies think just like daisies.

-Geraniums like geraniums. And finally… All and all, overall like flowers.

I am here, room of the ranch –I say to myself to convince myself-. I asked Ramon to lend it to me to rest. To come and meditate. To comprehend Teofila's death. Dear Teofila.

Beams on the roof, brass bed, bath covered with **Talavera** from Puebla.

-Actuality, the past has entered through the channel of deliriousness –the black viceroy comments, pointing his index finger.

-Past or no past.

-It couldn't have been past.

-Past in mind.

-Past of possibility.

-Who says we are not making things up.

-Who assures us that beyond these four walls we shall find the same elements from the past –the viceroys alternate phrases, playing again the mirror game. Suffer after metamorphosis converted in crows cawing: "Hemofiction, Hemofiction".

The image of the super-man came to my mind to receive immediately the horrendous sensation of conceiving myself as an inferior person –dominated by floral unconsciousness-, being stupid, governed by extra human forces –never extraterrestrial. Green conspiracy, secret. It can be considered that I am paranoid. It should result as our appreciation. Just like beatified terror pumpkins and apples.

I concentrate once again on the apparition. First as a body and then two viceroys that circumcised my experience, that they reduced and at the same time amplified, because the colony _New Spain- was introduced in the present time: hallucination in perfect coherence. If they were works of alcohol they would have turned into bulls or perverted angels and not only into miserable crows.

-Imaginations. The time of the colony and the present are the same. Temporary twins. The apple cuts during vice regal times; you eat it in the present and vice versa. To eat is to eat. We have eaten corn, which has turned into crows.

-Figurations. We have been animals of God. Damned figurations. The storm has released its waters over the immediate past. Noah just started yesterday his march, taking a pair of each animal of all species, including microbes.

-The people of flesh turn into animal flesh. Extreme guilt. You feather the past, Mr. Storyteller, why... why... just because.

-The people of flesh possess the privilege of refection –imitating the viceroys in their mirror game.

-Plants also think.

-Maybe plants can read? Could they write green philosophy?

-They don't need to: telepathy.

-As far as I know... Only God possess that kind of disrespectful penetration. We know that God sees all what happens and shall happen on the planet.

-God and the plants. They listen and read our thoughts. See our dreams. Guard.

-Two viceroys are. Two. Imbued like I of paranoia and feathers.

I wish to keep quiet and in peace. Drink without paying attention to the crows that caw on the windowsill.

-When you fell persecuted it's because… you intuit the green penetration.

-I feel, Mr. Viceroys, that time…

-The time is in its place. What has changed your consciousness, let's say, your way of taking it.

Once again both viceroys appear in front of me. Intellectual entities with mannequin definition. Black and white. Good and bad.

The secret lies hidden in the word HEMOFICTION –just as Teofila fell straight my brain introduce the scary repletion of the word for days and years.

-We are hemofiction –the viceroys assure, suspending for a moment their mirror game.

-And for so much mystery.

What kind of mystery? Teofila has perished and that meant HEMOFICTION, but also something else which didn't manage to distinguish. I had already aggravated her. She had bled. I dreamt it infinite times, I remember it now, that my room would fill with blood of my loved one. Warm blood.

-We also can't remember completely, only by parts.

Let's not reason to the matter. She was your girlfriend and not our. Teofila. The dead girl. The one you supposedly murdered yesterday or the day before yesterday. Here in the present or in another past.

I remember seeing the dead girl. Her mouth didn't pronounce the word but she said it.

-Hemofiction.

-Hemofiction, Teofila?

-Hemofiction.

That's when all dislocations of reality started and my daily metamorphosis of human to crow.

-Dislocations that you hadn't realized until now.

-Before you had seen yourself in the mirror like any other Christian that obeys certain rules, the same that assures everyday life. Tell me if you had ever woken up and turned the alarm clock of with your left hand. Tell me if you had never gone with your wife to the market. Tell me if hadn't ever gone to a concert or any theater show.

I said to myself, in front of the corpse: you shall turn into a crow, dear storyteller. Wings shall grow on your back. You shall croak.

I said that with no pain. No guilt. With absolute conviction. Instead of arms feathers. Instead of mouth, beak.

-That conclusion doesn't sound too logical. Crow that locks up man? Crow that wants to talk croaks?

-In reality it sounds illogical. People don't breathe in feathers suddenly.

-They don't suddenly croak.

-Not suddenly, with time, with time. With time – I yelled to the viceroys.

-Nobody will know that you killed her. Relax. Go and use the word relax in a very common sense to yours. Relaxation, because justice is asleep. The slayer sleeps. Those who never sleep are asleep...Those who watch...

-Vegetable soup voyageurs.

-Pumpkin flower soup followers.

-Green pot guard cake.

I said to myself: For society you shall remain impugn, but not for your spirit. Impunity? Why should I remain floating in impunity? Nobody who wasn't myself would like to remain impugn and guilty and for which would wish to pay sentence in jail, after being judged.

-That what you call spirit…. Floral consciousness… That what you call crime… guilty consciousness of crime… That what you call, in conjunction, having murdered little Teofila to revenge your father… That…is an invention. Like the possibility of becoming a crow –and in the act transforming into those animal abdominal croaking: "Hemofiction, Hemofiction".

The case, Teofila, the case… I'd like to be on top of the useless mysticism. Enter perfect frivolity. Far indifference. I don't feel a thing. I didn't do a thing because I don't remember it anymore. Impugn. Will my consciousness die? If so…precisely…I shall stop being a man and turn into a branch of an apple or pear tree. We know that I was innocent. We know about your father… he had to pay.

-The true case is, Mr. Storyteller, you started to get to know the mystery of the flowers. Did you or didn't you smoke marijuana? Did you or didn't you drink as a loved child? Well, then there's the mystery.

-What mystery are you talking about? You shall not say that you feel persecuted like Mr. Storyteller? –the white viceroy shows his teeth making fun in an atheist way.

I said to myself: If God transforms me into a crow I shall hate his divine body, I shall want his blood. I shall kick him. The divine Sir know what we drug addicts can do.

-New homely crucifixion. Jesus marches carrying his wooden saint. His hands and feet are once again nailed. Crown of spines –the white viceroy releases a crocodile's cry.

-Flowers concede metamorphosis. The vegetal kingdom can become crow, horse or centaurs. You wish to be penitent, let's say human. Flowers will wish to be tortured and not to ask for forgiveness and to regret, not that… -the black viceroy has become aggressive and slaps with his hand his half.

You purchase in the market a Christ and to continue… I take away my anger. Slap, slap, with the hand. He goes to the market again and buys a whip. Slap, slap. He buys a more simple one and slap, slap. This is what the benign Sir deserves for allying with the flowers.

-Wooden Christ inert. Sentimental Christ. Christ with *bugambilia* heart or poisonous mushroom. Deceitful Christ. Hadn't you saved us? Weren't we your children of predilection? Then, why does a crow come to some person's present and past story. Steps that don't hurt. Two steps and ascending to the feathers. Two steps down and man appears. With no pain. Without hope. Same head tested to same thoughts and history.

-Christ shall shortly start to bleed. Because sooner or later they are crucified. Spat. Puked on.

-Like tortured men. Paid as a crow. Confusion. Rum and beer hits me. The drinks have hit me and I wish to lie down. Dizzy? What is dizziness? –the white viceroy converted in crow, poses on top of the wardrobe and cries.

Mystery. Can we punish God and be happy? Mystery. I felt like locking myself up and hitting myself. I had gotten into the mood that nature gave me wings.

-It gives them. But yes. But yes. You fly, Mr. Storyteller. Right now I see beak instead of mouth. Feathers instead of wings.

Do you really know what nature is and on what side it stands?

I said to myself: condemnation. You shall be crow and person, animal and human, dirty and clean, two. Mother nature concedes miracles. Of course, Nature is on side of the… plants? Not that. Not that. Because that would mean that nature would be on an inferior level. It's because man is older than the plants and not the other way round. Oh dear Teofila, dear Teofila, save me and save yourself with me.

-And after, seeing the blood of the innocent girl spill you entered once again your reality, I mean, post-crime reality. Let's say, you left. You left or entered the reality? And what type of reality? First you love that person, then you murder her. After that, you relive such thing. You come here because you wish to pay for your sin that you ate before. Before what?

-You entered it, reality, through the same wrong door. You held your hand up, dear Teofila.

Premeditation, treachery and advantage. Because you had dreamt the crime. Let's say, that you had done it several times before being oneiric. You already carried the guilt then. You dragged that guilt as if it was a tail or wings back then.

-Latent threat: you shall turn into a crow –both viceroys cawed on the mirror, making the walls and the brass bed tremble.

That double prophecy will come true at the ranch. Why now? Mystery. Impossible to guess –the presence of the viceroys wanted to force the entrance of another age and the possibility that I were to be punished and redemption throughout the mentioned duality. Change of time. I will go to the colony and from the colony... God has no difficulties selecting his victims. He wished to punish Teofila's dad for drug dealing.

We are pulling you towards us. Can you feel it?

-Our presence weighs.

It had never occurred to me that the punishment for murder...Why return to the past? Why feather up in the past?

-Because we are the past and the past has feathers, you fly, Mr. Storyteller, you go from home to the bridge and from the bridge...

There supposedly was an independence and that New Spain…What do we carry in the blood?

-I think it's an imaginary accumulation. That heavy accumulation bursts with the ingestion of alcohol or unmeasured use of drugs. You burst.

-Imaginary accumulation –I say serving another Cuba with much rum and a lot of ice.

-I thought of imagination as a simultaneous reality.

-the reality that you think or imagine of is happening in a close dimension and remote at the same time.

-I am thought. I am what I think. What I would think of. What I will think.

-Exactly. We are thought of for other realities.

-Interferences. As if a radio station…

-Catches another signal.

-I am catching the past viceroyalty and my changed form. I'm man and animal. This deliriousness is starting to wear me out.

-Deliriousness?

-Yes, deliriousness, I think.

-I shall not stand against you. Think that the deliriousness which is, is or not deliriousness. Who cares? Experience is what matters.

-And she said, in front of Teofila's corpse that you shall turn into a crow.

Wings of crow. Evilness. Certain religious beliefs stat e that I once was an animal, so…

-So you can be one again, right? – inquires the black viceroy, sipping on his **cuba**.

-Animal chosen by crime. Blood which spills becomes a figure, like a sculpture. Created by an artist.

-Teofila's blood chose its mold: you shall be a crow.

-Teofila's blood said: you shall see your viceroys sooner or later. Maybe her blood even said you could invite us to drink with you and reconstruct your far and immediate past.

-You shall be punished by Mother Nature. She's angry. The lady Madam is pissed.

-How? How will I be punished?

-Addiction.

_I was an addict before committing murder. But I. But I.

-After addiction comes deliriousness. Have you started to be delirious? I bet you haven't.

-And the vagrancy of the vortex. You come and go and stay at the same site, firm with perversity.

-Sometimes you shall be human.

-And sometimes you shall become crow. Alternating animal and man.

-And after, alternating animal and plant.

-Sometimes crow.

-And some other times stem, flower.

Two found viceroys. Simple solution. If you don't fall from the right side... Coin in the air. Heads or tails? If I'm a man a while and afterwards a crow, who'll be able to throw the coin, or strong enough to throw me? God perhaps. The devil, maybe. The flowers?

-Adverse and reverse of the same.

-Coin in the air.

-Coin of your imagination.

-Face of Teofila.

-Back of Teofila.

Both viceroys, transformed into crows, cawing on the windowsill: "Hemofiction, Hemofiction).

I shall say beforehand that I am not catholic. I don't wish to be so. I shall say beforehand that I haven't behaved like a catholic. In that way…it won't be easy to close that bottle. Suspend the smoke. But I am anxious to get off. But yes.

A sea of thoughts has detached from the surging of the viceroys. It is said that alcoholics repress dream. May I have repressed so much oneiric material, to explore after nine years. The thing is to inquire from now, try to reach an improbable height –the thing is to denounce the complot of the flowers.

-Nobody shall believe you, Mr. Storyteller, not even us, you're mirrors, believe you. And why? Because belief is faith material. Air material. Immaterialibility. –the black viceroy starts to laugh out of amusement.

-Because nobody exists outside of these four walls. We're three and that's it.

-Maybe not even the walls.

-Have you gotten up to touch them?

-I have gotten up, yes. I have touched the walls with the palm of my hand –*I've touched them with my feathers.*

-But you have doubted whether the wall is a wall.

-I have doubted once, yes.

-Alcohol mediation the tact…

-Real bricks. Touchable reality.

-There must be a way to escape. I shall kneel down and ask for forgiveness. *Forgive me* –I yell, letting it all out.

Suddenly the evening gets dark and the Mr. Viceroys, changed as crows, close their eyes and sleep.

I also sleep and say to myself: Conscious of the conscious, perhaps –unstuck consciousness of vegetal hallucinations. Transcendental sense. Beyond the flowers must the human consciousness appear. Beyond the flora must find itself the road, which takes you to transcendence. Road. I bump into Jesus on the road. He carries the wood, which he'll be crucified on. Who are you, Mr.? I am the road and the life –responds Christ with absolute seriousness.

-Ingesting alcohol one can't reach the type of consciousness, on the contrary. Ingesting alcohol takes you on the road to degradation. On a slide. Towards the road of feathers –says the black viceroy.

-Drinking makes you reach the floral thought –sentences Jesus.

-Don't you find it logical? –white viceroy.

-I am here, here –Dimension where time and space mute just like insects do. Was I lost? Of course. I still am. Will I find the road? I doubt it. I know that I was born. I know that I was a baby with diapers. I know that I assisted to lower school and upper school. University and Music Conservatory. I know that the complot of the flowers took me into the alley of the murderous drug addict.

I received a suggestion on part of my wife and my cousin Ramon to get back to my senses through a times rest –they, of course, ignored what happened with Teofila. I accepted. Go to the ranch, said Ramon, there's no one there, only Anselmo, the caretaker –I could use that nobody as the receptor of my catharsis. Anselmo would be an inflamed person, of slow walking.

-Anselmo, magnificent ear.

-Anselmo, big ear.

-Listen to subtle insignificant things,

-Did you know Anselmo before coming or did you just imagine him?

-I didn't know him, nor imagine him. Ramon mentioned him to me. He said: the caretaker, just him. I the imagined the man attending the animals and cleaning the house.

-And the word became person. Your cousin mentioned Anselmo and that was enough for the man…

-Verb became flesh.

-Flesh of the caretaker from the ranch through the verb of your cousin. Powerful cousin Ramon.

Those are letters of visionary and not spelt –words of a killer in redemption. Road to something new towards something human. A deal to ascend towards the cross of salvation. The feathers of a crow shall fall some day. Some remote day I shall be able to fly in the sky with warm spirituality. For now…roam, drink, find out, go mad. It has been impossible to go back to my first reality. I have been conceived, nevertheless, not to fall in the duality Stem-Crow. Second duality. Second descend.

My father had threatened me in the bathroom of the house saying no to do anything bad otherwise I'll hit you. And if you do it, daddy? If you hit me you shall have black feathers of a demon. The commandments say: thy shall honor your father and your mother.

-And you honored the injections in the vein? I inherited that tendency.

-Can be.

-You doubt it?

-And who did I inherit, son, who?

Pages of round incoherency. Maybe you –somebody- finds ground to written present, useless revelations but surprising. Define uselessness as the illusion to frustrate the evilness of certain plants and flowers and the persistence of the universe –the cosmos shall extend its presence, but man...We shall keep on being born and dying –shall our reign last? Invented nature. Nests of scorpions proliferate between the holed walls of time. We shall continue. I shall write my memoirs and leave them to rest –time is broken to rest in my colonial corner, home of man and crow, warned division by the viceroys. But I come and go through time. Suddenly I find myself in the room of the ranch and suddenly in the old house in the road Republica de Colombia, a few meters away from the bridge that goes from onside to the other of the path behind San Pedro and

San Pablo. Somebody, like thou, shall read about my person and the viceroys which appeared to me –the may not believe. Maybe the reader belongs to the military submitted by the flowers. Shall read about Anselmo and Teofila, my other half. About my inability to escape –towards where? - from that monstrous conspiracy.

The phenomena —emergency and part of the viceroys —occurred in the ranch of my cousin Ramon —room to rest. I repeat with all the intention to stick to certain specific moments that escape from me, like anyone else. Sometimes I feel like filling twenty pages followed by these tow words: am here, because I barely distract myself since I call myself Santiago Amendola and find myself held back on the balcony of my house in ruins with a crow which is also my own person.

-Sometimes time becomes hard. The black viceroy knocks on the clock on the wall with his index finger.

-But sometimes it is soft and changeable, the time —the white viceroy moves his arms like a bird flying. Both look at the clock, sticking their eyes to the glass.

-Sometimes it becomes hard on the side where we appear.

-But sometimes in the colonial past.

-Old trace.

-Smell of gutter.

-Humidity

-How easy the face of time changes.

-If you come back —whispers the black viceroy, turning the hand of the clock back, and back...I am knowing that there is something else beyond these four walls... then you will the actual versatility.

-I shall go back to my old life. I shall be a normal person again. By law. Controlled by good. I shall walk on Jesus' road when I'll be forgiven. Feathers shall fall. Oh, I wish to feel, cry, but something... -I cover my face with the pillow, so I can start crying, but the tears are stuck in the tank.

-Fine decision, but it isn't voluntary your return. You shall have the opportunity to ask other delirious people about the problem. I am mentioning "others", there are possibly "others" like you.

-Others?

-Of course. Others.

-Supposedly I was...

-Supposedly an instant ago, but now... now the number of deliriousness has grown.

Please, the reader ascends to the second floor of any building and from there he warns of what we have turned into –*open your minds and listen to the internal voice of the specie.*

-Specie. Exteriority. Community. Society.

-Beehive –the bees have lost the talk and with talk the reason to specialize in extreme actions. Are the bees drugged and for that...?

-Extreme actions like human actions. Eat. Drink. Go to the movies. Watch T.V. Comment the news, the same with the same news... White news and white movie. Nothing –the two viceroys have sat on the footboard of the bed after turning on the television, which doesn't tune into any program: black rays and incoherent sounds.

There we go. We read the same book We laugh at the same joke. *There we go.* We are members of an identical church and eat from the same plates –tendency towards the can-opener, adultery of tortillas and milk. Tendency to depreciate what is really makes pleasant a stay on a planet. Tendency, which governs one party and further on one nation. Mathematical movements. *–Are you still watching dear reader(s)?* Out of six talkers in the building –anybody, in any neighborhood –at least two individuals which call themselves human deal drugs and another two use them and the fifth one makes them –lucrative action has released itself from the legal and medical purpose. To be a pro-elite drug dealer is the maximum dream of any middle class. I don't blame anyone –I mean, human. Mental weakness. God made us that way. Easy to convince. Easy to drag.

-I would gladly try an injection. You inject and forget. Goodbye duties. Goodbye consciousness. Goodbye –whispers the black crow, posing on top of the wardrobe.

-In exchange, I abominate them. I think the church is enough. I believe one live under the yoke of the parents comfortably. That's what I think. I think as I am. White viceroy. It's good to go to the cinema and watch white movies. It's good to assist to church and pray even though you don't believe in God –the white viceroy has managed to tune in a program on the TV set, it seems like a soap opera, but we still can't here what the actors are saying, always close to crying.

-You and I pray. You and I go to the cinema. If we leave this place we shall work and maintain our family like good suppliers. To be a supplier is not shame, on the contrary, I start to feel pride. The older son comes and asks for school. Go ahead, son, pay the school –and we shall extend a check in the name of the school of the teaching priests. Comes the younger son and asks for toys, of course yes, we shall go to the toy store on the day of your birthday –on TV a silent advertisement of some toy is shown.

-We look like two people not known to the storyteller –the viceroy-crows touch their hands, shoulders, their head and feet.

-We don't seem that because we are.

-Not always. But no. But no.

-We could say in few words why we're in this room?

-Because yes- I say just before turning into a crow.

-Good answer. Because yes. Nature invents –it is true. Nature spawns strange fish, affirms the program on TV.

I fly to the back of the room and return to get comfortable on the pillow.

-Nature says: because I make dogs bark. Because if the earth quakes. Because volcanoes spit lava -*it is true, volcanoes throw up lava.*

-You are talking about the world that exists beyond these four walls. Am and was, existed throughout time. Things happened to me before. I killed and regret. Oh, my Teofila, how I wish to kneel down and cry –I talk with the beak and not with my mouth.

-That's right. Now that world exists, but it didn't exist until... how long?

-It appeared on the television. We suddenly saw it there, in a box.

I was bursting when I arrived at the ranch –alcohol and bitter remorse, deep, in legion, numbing my dreams. Explosion. My pieces shall tell my past, but especially about my present –hope to reverse the vegetal conjure. But yes. I shall be an unlock agent someday. Someday I shall get on the bus trying to convince anyone to follow the road of my consciousness, go towards the spirit. But no, because I would have to suspend the ingestion of alcohol before.

Next to the end, drunk, I had lied on the brass bed of that new room –or old. Place where I had gone to seek shelter from my crisis and depression –I can't tell the difference. Now I doubt whether I've spent some time submerged in the vortex. Now I doubt about the ranch and think about my wife Canuta and my cousin Ramon, they have locked me up in a madhouse. But no. But no. There are no nurses and psychiatric doctors marching.

Be part of it. I am. Be torn into a thousand pieces. Who could protect and build oneself an identity. Be Peter or John, lawyer or salesperson. Somebody defined.

The language of the flowers and plants turns out incoherent. They create images and situations. Send to the madhouse consumers and producers that feel like kings, prepared individuals and not idiots. The start gangs here and there. Take entire neighborhoods.

-Did you say madhouse?

-Place where there are mad people.

-Instead of putting me into one of those sites, my wife wanted to…

-Repair your head. Remember your nervousness. Your pulse trembled. You couldn't even hold a glass of alcohol to cure your hangover. Thank your prudence. Thank your mouth that it has kept quiet about your crime. Because if she knew… Because if she could imagine… We couldn't get a thing with the doubts of your wife about your possible lost identity. She may start to suspect… Can you imagine what she would imagine?

I had been feeling bad for quite some time. I had told Canuta, Like never before, nervous, close to an irremediable crisis. Take me to the doctor. I ignore whether she… Did she take me? Put a foot in the madhouse? Not at all. Put a foot into another reality. I mean, one of healthier individuals than I. Follow the footsteps and imitate the others. Footsteps of health. Where? In the ranch of my cousin Ramon. I say it and repeat it. Because yes. I find myself here. I shall rebuild that broken down person.

-We all felt a desire to leave. Desire to talk. Desire to drink. So we left to chat with you. You have the obligation de keep us informed who you are, what you do, what good and bad you've in life.

Drug dealers wish to be important –I say before drinking another cup of tequila.

-They wish to serve the flowers in exchange of houses and risk. Those wishes come true. They buy houses. Deposit money in the banks. Corrupt families introducing them to the business. Cell brings gained cell. Inside and outside the government. Outside and inside the police and the army. Idiots can be everywhere.

-Why did you come to the ranch Mr. Storyteller? As far as I know you should have gone to the madhouse and never leave that place. You enter and greet all the men dressed in white with a silly smile and they return your courtesy by locking you up in a padded cell. In four walls, just like here. Four balls where we were born.

It became more frequent the tendency of not showing up to work.

-Normal. Up to there I see it as normal... Continue –says the black viceroy just before turning into a crow and putting its claws on the footboard of my bed.

-Human production shall cease. Factories shall stop. Clocks will become unreadable.

-Apparently this shall happen –I say, serving a cup with the remaining tequila.

-Apparently this shall happen in the mind of every delirious man.

-Overpopulation in the madhouses –I say, putting the cup on the night table, after taking a few sips.

-In the madhouses, of course. Continue.

After exchanging a few words with my wife Canuta I started to pack. Under the advise of my cousin Ramon I left behind the resignation of my job and asked for a permit without receiving salary. My wife agreed. She would try to avoid the threat –turning into a crow and paying for the murder of little Teofila.

-Subjective menace.

-Floral.

I got on the bus with passengers and slept for two hours *–dreamt that I was standing on a mast of a bridge made out of wood. I tried to warn the neighbors of the threat of the flowers, but instead of words, croaks came out of my beak. The bells marked twelve midnight. I fly up to the balconies of the house of Don Santiago Amendola. I enter and see the man sleeping. An immense anger takes over me, which makes search for a whip. God is guilty. God – like my dad- deserves to be hit. I shall drink his blood.*

-Real dream.

-True dream

-You turned into a crow without knowing.

-Without knowing that you shall turn into a stem. Continue.

I bought at the station some bottles of tequila and arrived at the ranch quite drunk, where I really needed to rest.

-You have mentioned the ranch a hundred times. We don't see a ranch, just walls. Four walls.

Anselmo opened the room. I took out the clothes and tidied the wardrobe and drawers.

-And then comes the clothing, if we are not mistaken.

-They're still there. You haven't used them.

-Because you haven't even taken a bath.

I got comfortable on the bed and kept on drinking and in a wink of an eye the viceroys appeared. How many hours have you remained here? Days? Light has changes, but… But yes. It is possible that two or three weeks have gone by, dialoguing with them, my equals.

-Us two. Two concrete people.

-In exchange of cries I spilt two tears –a true young crying feeling, adolescent. The matter is that I do not remember why- Why did I cry? For her. My dear Teofila. Because I was précised to confess.

-And afterwards?

Time. While I was fleeing what I did(n't) want to confront had reached me –I still couldn't see nor have the intuition of the face of my enemy.

-Of course you knew it.

-Of course you had seen it in your true dreams. Of course. But sure, man, you remember. Even Teofila knew about your trips of deliriousness. She warned: if you keep having more you shall end up crazy, locked behind four walls. As far as I know she did it on many occasions. I suppose it was because the girl loved you.

-You were supposedly going to get married with her? If that is so… well, she would have had to understand that your second matrimony would be illegitimate. Canuta is your second wife…

The mandatary lords would stand in front of me, but they were independent, they'd rule from their own will *—we have believed until now the vegetal reign lacks of movement and speech. And if through their veins runs chlorophyll and not blood?*

-Let us ask: where did we really come from, can you tell us? Of course not. We ignore it, but so do you. Human character. Maybe the flowers know.

It had surged from me the constant question. Inversed continue. Backwards. We are going back to the past and towards the future. From the car came the carriage pulled by horses or donkeys. Is it true that I got married with Teofila or was she simply a childish girlfriend? The second probability is more common…

-Where did we come from, can you answer? If we should have come out all slimy out of the belly of a woman like you did… we wouldn't know either. If we would have been slimed for floral reasons, as you assure, then, we would be dumb. Total ignorance. For one and another reason. From a belly or without a belly. Of woman or of man the birth is unexplainable. Mystery. Hemofiction.

You two were born from my constant silence over the murder –I felt guilty, that's why I felt like fleeing. They are, if I misunderstand, children of this accumulated feeling or choked in my interior. I ignore why another viceroy was born after the first one. I do not know that. Because I could have easily threw him up myself. But the reason…the reason I do know, the crime.

-Are you sure of the crime?

-Sure of its evilness yes, I am.

-Teofila fell to the ground.

-The one who was to be my wife wanders through time.

-Was I pregnant and that's why…?

-No, no, not because of that, it was because of the father.

-Legitimate father-in-law. Soldier father-in-law. Military. You came through the front door of the house and…you attacked. Crime.

I committed it as I was barely a kid –drunk attack on Teofila. Silence. Burial of that strange revelation to my character. –would it be possible that I was that bad and that evilness revealed itself in such a strong way from one moment to the other? I left myself and did what I today consider impossible, since it hasn't repeated again –supposedly the tendency towards evil governs over the bad.

-Who supposes that?

-It has been deduced with the experience of bad people.

-Constant assassins.

-Yes, assassins repeat.

-Not all repeat, there are many like you that don't do such thing again.

-Minor guilt.

-O major, depending on the angle how it is viewed. You could have controlled yourself, or not?

-Yes, I could.

-So then you are guilty under the eyes of God than the one who sins for irremediable reasons.

I have been and am an individual more inclined to good. Relatively good. I avoided to hand out money but wasn't a thief, not really. Anger could possess me but I was incapable of killing. I am never nor under any condition saying that I committed murder with treachery and advantage –I did the act, of course I did I am talking about my existence after this act –I stopped being the one I was just to do such absurd deed which couldn't be me. I lived being one until before the crime and afterwards I returned to be the same after committing it. Interruption. Evil short circuit that doesn't match.

-Matched for a second. Long instant. Past or coagulated time in your psyche. Chiseled image. One that runs the same way next to the other. Now I start to understand. How the image became parallel to the time giving force to our double birth. Because each images has its adverse and reverse. Two faces of the coin, we said it before. Two faces found of the fact that remained petrified in your interior. You enter and exit yourself but stumble on what bugs you all the time, I mean, yourself.

-Brief or long, it's the same to me. You were right with the evil. To run parallel with him. You are yourself and the other, the fractured during the concrete fact.

-And you immediately were the one you had been for nine years of gestation. Nine of keeping us in your mind and heart.

-Nine years of lock up.

-The vomit had to happen. It had to.

-You are talking casually. I didn't have to happen as it happened. On the contrary. It happened just because; we've commented this before. Because yes this man-individual went home to his girlfriend and killed her. Because he had smoked marijuana. Because yes the evil train continued marching on the side of its original to turn suddenly into, into the absolue present, in three: original and two copies in black and white.

-Then the man got into the ordinary. I say he entered to keep the course of his days as if nothing had happened. The case is, the tumbled cart stayed behind the personality.

-It stayed, it stayed cawed the viceroy-crows.

I talk about my sunken existence in common worries –pay electricity and telephone, buy meat and vegetables for the refrigerator, see the last movie. Read the last fashionable novel. Drowned existence in the diary: school, home, friends, recent girlfriend and later work and marriage –the face of the enemy followed each one of my movements, because it marched next to me. Inside and beside, at the same time. Absolutely parallel which affected this present also absolutely where many diverse pasts and futures exist.

-You should say the each one of your movements seem normal until before exploding. Until before you allow us enter these four walls of the ranch.

-Movements that hit and skip when they bruise Teofila's presence.

-Does that past action seem real?

-It was real for the non-delirious.

-Tomorrow and the day after tomorrow I shall come back to reason. I shall recover my sane judgment. I swear. Tomorrow I shall stop drinking. I shall put out the joint.

-It is very unlikely that that will occur. Because once time explodes... Because once a personality explodes... Because once you are inside and to the disposal of the flowers...

Material –when somebody murders someone blood comes out, we see the corpse. The corpse fell in front of me. I saw blood. It flowed. Red.

-We imagine the corpse of Teofila lying and squirting blood. We can easily imagine that.

-Imagine the stream of blood and the squirt coming out of the head but it does not wet, but does not stick on tact.

-We sure can see the corpse. Yes. But we can't see her real face. Teofila is one for us and another for you.

-Her real body. One for us and another for you.

There was then –arms and legs, head, long hair. Concrete body. Exterior and interior flesh –guts. Black shoes. Dressed with black and white points –those points turned into two angry viceroys.

-Of course not.

-Points found. Of course not.

-You have seen too many movies.

-You have watched too much TV. Let's say, the non-existing has penetrated you like marrow in a bone.

-Televised respiration.

-Eat news.

-You talk about Teofila and not about black and white points.

That being –that delicious young girl- I took away her smile –then she was drugged, she had smoked marijuana.

-Well, suddenly the truth comes out, a certain motif. She had smoked. But not all who smoke kill. But not all have killed Teofila, or yes? Differences. Let's see them. Let's at least try to distinguish them between a pothead and another. Between an alcoholic and another.

-Had you smoked.

-And that is why you became pregnant with us.

-And that's why you find yourself stuck between these four walls.

-Stuck a few hours. I know that this drunkenness shall pass, like others. I know I shall come back to sane judgment, I said so. My mother awaits it. My wife Canuta is waiting. Even Teofila's spirit awaits it.

Too much waiting.

Two much time locked in two hour of deliriousness. You know, plants and flowers are not interested how things go by nut just all internal, I mean, the steps of deliriousness, I mean, the flow of images, river of past and present consciousness, future and present.

-You talk about little Teofila.

-You try to justify yourself.

-You still need to tell us the reason.

I took away the perverse caresses of her dad –he had snorted cocaine. I took away the love of her father –because he was smoking.

-Where did you get such…? I mean the coke.

Outside school, supporters of the enemy sold it. Beings that walk in vegetal state.

I took Teofila's birthday presents away, Christmas too. Hurt dead. Died immediately. Now she lives and now she dies. You take your time saying it. Disgusted face that remains on the face. Accusation –surprise face and meaning: it wasn't possible that I… It wasn't possible that you… Past. Forgot about the incident and dedicated myself to keep on copying the others –zero drugs, zero alcohol.

-But you already were nuts, mister storyteller, you had climbed the necessary steps to start feathering and cawing.

-The word floral has been planted.

I was surprised, no matter, the internal necessity of bursting of so much time that I transformed myself into a normal person –I even went to church on Sundays. I had managed to erase the miscarriage of my personality.

-Bad people are not meant to go to church.

-Listen to mass.

-Assist. Enter church. Kneel down. Pray.

-When the march of the train is found.

-Train, which shall crash.

What was happening with me? I conserved myself insensitive to the fact. Let's say, it was easy to cry without feeling remorse –the ones that sold and sell drugs outside schools don't have any remorse either, have they been dominated against their will by something superior, deep face that I have seen in dreams, immense mouth constructed with gardens, roses, azaleas, snow drops, daisies, poppies…

When the characters popped up I said to myself: That's what should have happened. I already knew it. Yes.

-Yes, like that.

-The viceroys already existed.

-We were spawned.

-Together with the death in house of your father-in-law, the main drug dealer and long pregnancy.

-During that bloody fornication they were conceived and born.

-Poor you, Teofila.

-Well, the pity, pitying yourself. I also pity.

-Mirror of compassion.

-Reflection of pity.

-Common light that doesn't touch the dead.

-Do you wish to touch her? Do you dream that you touch her?

-Then it happened that we appeared on the time that repeats, on the time that goes back and forth and vice versa.

-We appeared and…

I said: That is the most logical thing in the world. Now that you saw them I asked myself why they hadn't appeared them before. As a matter of fact, I had already wanted to talk to them at the park.

-And why not.

-How was it or did Teofila's death happen? You have managed to integrate us.

I remember: I left the house –hers, the dead-, after staying there quite while under the shower –part to get rid of the dumb state and part to wash the traces and blood. Talking a bath I said to myself: the planted bean needs of water in abundance. For some reason I closed my eyes and thought about the story of the magic beans. Absolutely wet. I used once and again the soap on myself and ran down the road for a while –the beanstalk would follow my intelligence, twisting my growth inside my cranial warehouse. Under the influence of drugs I said to myself: you have treaded that place always inhabited by the dead and there was a flowerpot that was flourishing. I am in the present and the other...past is.

-You shall never go back.

-Never.

-Never go back.

-Never

-But you saw the flowerpot.

-And the bean was growing.

-Outside the pot and inside you're the head.

I waited to get dry and presented myself at home as if nothing had happened.

-Hi Ma, Hi Dad –And I went to hide under my pillows –ferocious laurel roots pushed into my vigil dreams.

-Does your tooth hurt? –asked Mom.

Yes, a lot, as if I had killed someone.

Let me get some aspirins.

-Thanks, I'd rather have a cup of tequila, beer or something that dazes.

-What are you running from, son?

-I think I'm running from you, Mom, from home. From something that I do not understand. I have had dreams... I have seen... It wasn't a face and nevertheless...

-You talk about evil.

-But I am not talking about the devil but...I think...I am thinking that perhaps the flowers... You see, I've been for years letting leaves and roots and flowers grow in my dreams. Bugambilias and geranium, snowdrops and ivies with juvenile airs. As if my head was a flowerpot –there's one in the house of my girlfriend Teofila.

-You love her?

-Yes, I love her.

-Does she water your pot?

-Sure, she waters it daily.

Several red notes appeared proving the fact of innocent people: drug dealers that wanted to make adjustments with the father of the dead.

Time went by and I didn't mention anything on what had happened –neither talked about my green dreams. Silence. Forgot –the red eyes of a thousand insects flirt in my interior, invite me to get closer to the world of the plants, where it is possible to murder in infinite creative forms. Here, suggest the eyes, you can be beautiful and cruel.

-Let's go back to the beginning –suggests the white viceroy.

-You locked yourself up in this ranch.

-Why do we call these four walls a ranch?

-Once again I found myself in front of these two beings –made by myself –flesh of my flesh. Incarnated abstractions.

-Hello, good day.

-Good night.

-Or good afternoon, Mr. Storyteller. Could you refer to us how you appeared here?

I had an intuition about this place, faraway; I could see up close the vegetal face of power –reason to the addiction and the idiotism of the dealers- the reason for my continuous chlorophyll dreams.

I try to get up and go to the bathroom but I can't. I close my eyes. Dizziness. I fall in the vortex of black feathers; I am a crow once again.

I know that hangovers make you hallucinate –ecstasy during the first moments and horror after, for example: the naked lady that has appeared to seduce us gets vampire fangs and immediately runs after us as a spider; the angel transforms into a demon, the dog into a bull, smells rotten what before smelt like perfume…

-Teofila's crime smells rotten to me –assures the white viceroy, swinging the sinister hand in front of his nose.

-Because she became rotten.

-Because she is becoming rotten.

-Because in the floral world she continues to decompose.

-Green images.

-Images-root.

-Impossible to pull out.

Sober, drunk or hung over, the viceroys would have appeared sooner or later. Product of guilt? I doubt it. I didn't feel guilt. In reality, I didn't feel anything, besides anxiety, for the obsession. Constant hammering of an imaginary pin above my temple. Teofila. Teofila. Loud beats that tried to be mystic. Supposedly these absurd and consistent beats, I should knee in front of any image by hand and spill out a hot and splendid cry.

-Do you regret?

-I hope so.

I wouldn't. The anger dictated different acts and in some cases even violent. Feel like shaving people. Feel like cutting their nails way too short.

-Do you regret?

-Regret what I did?

-Of course you did it.

-You have recognized your guilt.

-Well, I don't recognize a thing. I never knew little Teofila and her father even less, the military man.

-Sit down and tell. Spit it all out. It's time to let it all out. Have you come in tone of judgment? Misters, I dream of a face composed of herbs, an immense vegetal mouth. I shall go to the madhouse after this. I may be crazy. It may even be that the crime isn't true –it is, the bean grows which represents guilt. Their little stems start to grow and get fat. I have fallen into domination –I am of the vegetal. The plants are taking revenge on us and God has allowed them to.

-Did you secretly marry Teofila? If so…it is not valid.

-I didn't get married with her, but…I would have a thousand times in love.

As a child I told dad: it is not possible that in the garden and the squares and the forests and next to the rivers those tremendous roots would grow which are shown to anyone.

-Tell us something about the image of the dead girl. Tell us about her roots —ask the albino crow from the wardrobe.

The dead girl would go with me to all places.

-Teofila's portrait covered with blood.

-It supposedly. I suppose. I talk coherently and incoherently a certain time. I go towards the viceroy-crow and towards myself. Internal and external public. I ask myself if those beings are out of blood or out of chlorophyll.

-We bleed if you stab us.

-Green blood.

Under the superficial consciousness where I could smile and communicate like any other individual I winked always the image of the dead girl —and the leaves of a plant that grew in her house, green and shiny, so much that it made me thirsty. Teofila watered that plant, vital drops of water every afternoon.

-O.K., I'll confess, I haven't forgotten her —neither the plant. Correct, I regret what I did —in that flowerpot red beans were growing. Her beans. She became a plant herself, root, green image. Vortex mirror where I find myself. Where I have fallen. I'll go.

-More that regretful, we se you scared. Logical. Falling inside and see that face that you mention... see from up close the face of evil.

-Because inside....deep inside

-Inside

-What we usually call inside...

-The image of the winking girl.

-wink.

-She gets up and walks. She has resurrected. She walks in the gardens of your soul.

Close flirting eye. Out of the pupil of my girlfriend comes a bean sprout. It grows. It dances to the rhythm of a snake.

-Here I am, Mr. Storyteller, this is what you did –talks Teofila –Do you prefer black or light beans?

Did I make her grow stems instead of worms?

-The image went down in your internal lake –the albino crow utters from the heights of the wardrobe.

-The image swims in your insides.

I went with her always –seaweed hands, agglomeration of irises.

-You're exploding. You shall go up to the sky. You shall see God. It is green and powerful. Do you truly regret?

Understand that I was high, Teofila. Understand the flowers… -to dream so much wears one out. The flower in the pot is sprouting even if nobody is watering it. The bean is growing marvelously from your blood.

-Mr. Storyteller, Are you suggesting that the whole specie shall end up high?

-I have seen the face… face of God, immense God.

-Face-Flower.

-Face-Plant

-Do you remember me? My name is Teofila Tejocote, at your service. I am the daughter of the general that has my same last name. The man has won in the battle of daughter love. The man awaited me to go pure to matrimony. Dressed in white. Happy and in communion.

-Yes, Teofila, I remember.

-I keep myself virgin for you. I conserve myself moist, raising moss.

Until the day of my wedding her image beat during the ceremony without anyone suspecting –I forbid flowers in the church.

-The image grinned, reminding you that she was your legitimate wife.

-The image beat, pointing out the lack of correctness.

-Tiny little beans grow out of the flowerpot while you were cumulating. Do you accept Canuta as your wife…? I am a widow, I accept.

Stoplight, bloody –body laying face up. I hadn't thought that the position could turn into accusation. Teofila, I said to her while I was receiving the rings next to Canuta, please sleep sideward or face down.

In the mouth of the dead girl grew a rose, spines down the throat.

-Hemofiction, Hemofiction –I can hear myself, cawing.

Teofila, you have white teeth and dark hair. Daughter off General Carlos Tejocote. Fat. Despot. Dirty. I had seen him many times on TV as military –agent to the flowers- arguing transparently and honestly, pretending to be a white dove.

-Your father is evil, Teofila.

-He's a sun when he appears.

On weekends the man would disappear with his main family, the first one.

-Your father has two families.

-Yes, he's married to the army.

-With the consciousness of the flowers.

-I don't understand, what are you accusing him of?

—He serves another specie.

-Green man.

The evil man would take them to the movies and tell them lies about his absences during the week.

He worked a lot for that... Soon... tomorrow...the army will need me... Mr. Tejocote would say.

-Your father support drug dealing.

-If you wish to be my friend, Mr. Storyteller, do not talk badly about my father.

Towards that person with twisted declarations to the press and TV.

-Crusade against vices. Crusade against consumers, producers and distributors.

Listening to one of his speeches he had come to do the idea to convince him of his violent error. I shall kill your daughter so that he suffers –what remains of his humanity shall rise. Small egg on the back of the animal –the death of Teofila shall unhook him, I think, out of the stupidity that the flowers have submerged him into.

I came out of my own speech the urge to act strangely to me –I shall rot in a few minutes, I shall be like General Tejocote: dual personality, double family, but at the same time different: beneficial murderer against the floral influence.

Then I said to myself, boy: since the general pretends, I can also pretend –in reality my dreams are starting to poison me, in reality I have those complex vegetal moments, chlorophyll thoughts.

I supposed that this version of pretension was valid. I had a motive: to save mankind from the floral influence.

I went to the mirror and repeated so theatrical lines. I shall take revenge with you, honorable lord, I said to Mr.Carlos Tejocote. You are the essence of the army and the essence of the young –essence is a bean stem, incomprehensible twist. I hope the reader perceives my anguish.

Consumed the vengeance would give my triumph –the bean stem had surged such a mad idea.

-You came to your sense.

-I'll come.

-Because today is yesterday

-Do you expect redemption?

I am willing to lose a hand or a leg. Now I understand the words of Christ: if your hand is cause of sin...

-Go ahead with the crime, please.

The best disguise for a bastard is innocence.

-You are innocent before committing a sin.

I would disguise the bastard only for seconds and immediately return to cover myself in moral codes learnt at home –the lesson to general Tejocote lacked of scientific explanation.

-And of sense.

-And of organization.

This was the plan: infringe unbearable pain to get back the human face to the father of my girlfriend.

-Great plan.

-Pain makes Christians.

-Of course.

But we talk about moral pain.

-Of course.

-The human general would be your equal.

-Storyteller and general brotherhoods.

-Both shall dress in black. Both shall cry for the human loss.

-Two united, venerating Teofila forever, against the floral conspiracy. It wasn't like that- The presence of Teofila went beyond the project –she became a vegetal memoir herself. Mr. Carlos Tejocote remained together with the drug dealers and I maintained myself insensitive until the apparition of the viceroys.

-Are you talking with a possible reader or us?

-I don't talk, I write.

I met her in the road. Greeted. Hello, Mr. Storyteller. Hello Teofila, do you want to be my girlfriend? If you don't start with kisses, sure.

U consider people like thinking blocks that only shall separates them the fantasy of being different –and by the way, every day we shall be less different.

-And more delirious, by the way.

Everyday we shall listen that there are more that dream with vegetal twists.

-Thousands and even millions of delirious people shall find themselves in the vortex.

Even though my head doesn't work, sometimes I do read newspapers and novels –in them I discover and point out the influence of flowers. In them I identify traces of my parents. I don't know what scientist said, implicating that humanity runs ahead millions of years, that we are cousins to the trees, he was wrong: the trees have evolved more than men have, to such extent that their roots fatten dreams.

At the end, they are naked on the bed –much time after what happened to Teofila-, in the ranch of my cousin Ramon, I decided to take out myself the viceroys: black and white viceroy, dialectic, move myself to separate –per pathetically- towards the comprehension.

-Now it turns out that you took us out and with a defined purpose.

Meiotic modesty. The decision to provoke the exit of the two mandataries that have been in my existence for quite some time before arriving to my site of rest –one thing is to suffer, another is to give birth. A similar impulse to the need of throwing up what was rotten in my interior and threw it to the back of the room. Urge to find out. I should die knowing.

-You'll see. The alcohol confuses time, which is the main effect. Do you agree?

I could go drinking to breakfast meetings at work and hold long conversations with clients, always giving them the reason –the reason is next to the executives, the ones that pay.

-I laugh to keep the client happy.

-I laugh to please: yes, Mr. Boss, yes, you're right.

-Yes, yes, Mr. President.

-Yes, yes, Mr. Priest.

-It could be said that the door were opened to the irrational.

-You entered the ranch of your cousin Ramon and…

While we are willing to concede reason to others, success shall smile at us. Do you realize my language of publicist? I am repeating things that have no importance, but I must rush –anguish, the vegetal mouth fills my being with green movements, rivers of chlorophyll, dark springs that smell of flower. I feel followed. Urged to close the circle of my memoirs.

-For us close and reappear at the moment that you enter the house general Tejocote.

-For us go back to the moment that you beat the blood of your girlfriend.

I see the crow –the same- stepping puddles of blood. I try to fly but am stuck.

II

THROUGH THE DOOR

At the main house of the ranch, there was nobody. Outside: Pigs grunted. Crickets could be heard. Frogs here and there. Unquiet nights because of the strong rainstorms, washing the leaves of the trees, flowers, plants. Anselmo Moratines, the caretaker, came to knock at my door and asked:

-Is everything alright, Mr. Storyteller? I hear noises and feel very unsteady. Lately my sensitivity has been very high and everything seems to be highlighted. I suddenly feel like the frogs and pigs have become quiet and that the leaves are becoming to be a threat. Will I get feathers and start to caw? Or shall I fall in the silence of the flowers?

-Everything is alright, Anselmo –I respond transformed in a crow-, except my slight drunkenness that is making me see things double, except that now I understand that certain flowers and plants do to us.

-They want us back because they love us, green lovers, dreams that caress my dreams with their soft petals. I wake up hung over seeing in front of my eyes a rose.for example, and I think it came out of my ears.

-Can I be sincere and let out a little madness without frightening you? Thanks, Buddy. Here it comes. Let me start: Two hemispheres. Conscious and food poison. Eatable plants and... Little by little you shall start to comprehend. There are vegetarian junkies and...we've been fighting inconsistently form thousands of years. Tubercles and stems in proliferation. Dream the mouth of such being...Metaphysical suction, spiritual absorption. Conflict. Conflictive. Bad if we'd create the kings of the creation. Bad if we'd think that we are superior to the plants and animals. Good and bad. God-Nature. The ambivalence prevails in the vegetal and mineral world. Masculine-Feminine. We have believed to be alone... and... They... It seems that we are losing.. It sounds like war, right? Well, it's been declared since... I have lost. I accuse the plants, because I affirm... Major complot –Marijuana is not innocent and... neither are the ones that consume and distribute her. What's the point of putting her into jail? Who's going to put the jungle into jail? I see that I am talking way ahead of time. I see once again that my consciousness... Great part of it... if not most of the people... doesn't recognize the enemy, it hasn't been found, only at superficial level –I smoke to be happy. That can be heard in this or that house, during parties or sleep. Happy or gone? Church doesn't help. Government even less. The polish the silly sects next to the bandits and dealers, next to absorbed bureaucrats and professionals –Teofila may have finished under the dominion of some fake saint, I say myself to lighten up the guilt that I carry with me. She died catholic, advantage. She died thinking about superiority of the specie. At the end, I come to the present that remains for me, lapses in space and time that tomorrow...

Bugambilia branches have entered the room.

-Keep quiet and more clearly, please –begs Anselmo-. A big hole has opened in me that wishes to express peace, silence and vegetal blindness.

-Would you believe that the tequila has made two viceroys appear in front of my own eyes? I am talking about now, Anselmo... subjective time. New Spain has acquired a presence in this subjective time that beats in the depths of all Mexicans, y your depth and in mine that, in reality, is the same depth. Did you know that back then there were many ghost stories and **pulquerias**? I disapprove much mud, dead cats and dogs in the streets, just as a gut remover of the animals at la Plaza Mayor, and pig breeding. Sales people that half dressed drink water from the fountains just like the beasts. It smells like rotten blood, rotten meat, rests of rotten food. I stink myself, stench of months not bathing. In that space and time –different than now- I call myself Santiago Amendola and crow, the people assure that I am two in one, feathered animal and evil person, friend of bandits and miserable ones. Permanent drinkers visit my house in ruins: holes in walls, furniture, carpets, penetrations of weeds and geraniums. Chipped dishware. Secret room where there's a suffering Christ locked up which opens his eyes when I hit him. Transpersonal voyage. Let's underline that some psychiatrists use psychotropic to accomplish motion towards lives before. Are you there Anselmo, have you moved towards colonial times with me and start to see the carts and boats full of vegetables?

-I shall leave you with your drinks; I have a lot to do –and things that I do not wish to do, wish to enter on Sundays forever without church, taking care of my hangover. I have reproached God once having created a week worth of labor, I envy the roses that don't have to do a thing to make their life. I feel that I am listening to you, Mr. Storyteller. I shall end up shattering that romantic image that I hold in those times where the adventures with cape and sword… when the fine maids of purgatory… where the inquisition… where the thousand bridges that cross the fields…. Where the cries are heard from Casa de Cabildo and Counties… Where they play dices and cards and drink on long tables and taverns… Even I, by fortune, haven't reached the accumulated pestilence in the center of Mexico. My parents were clean people, like the Indians, they bathed daily because daily…I soaped myself twice a day and twice let the water in the shower flow. I run, goodbye, I leave because I am becoming curious. I feel a certain internal necessity with you to throw scabby confessions.

-Goodbye, Anselmo, God bless you –I say flying to the door at the room. Through the crack, A geranium branch has sneaked in, threatening.

-God bless me, but I want to hear.

-God, it is said, doesn't make distinction between social classes. Loves the dark, just as much as he loves the white. Gives full hands to the poor and to the rich. There's no doubt of that- During Colonial times he advised the priests: keep your churches clean, avoid the unclean to empty with food and animals spreading fleas. Don't allow the women to talk about sex in the confessionary. As a matter of fact, in any place is bad… It sounds bad that a lady… The sex, following Tolstoi, Kreuzer sonata, must be used exclusively to conceive, never for pleasure. The bride shows the white dress in total coldness. Receives the male penis from the cold man. In exchange, the product is to be worshipped from the same moment of conceiving with perfect idealness.

-Human exaggerations, anxieties for perfection, lack of knowledge, ignorance.

-Thousand of wasted erections.

-The cold woman pushes the man to adultery, Mr. Storyteller. We stand against adultery no matter how romantic it seems and against the crime –say the friars-. And since stand against… they open eternal prisons where they pull out their nails, pump their stomachs, break their bones and teeth.

-I shall have to moderate myself if I don't wish to be burned. But then, I shall have to stop drinking and that…

-Criminal consciousness of man. I am criminal.

-Criminal who has killed?

-Mirror to other men who are delinquents. Mirror to some men that give their backs to Jesus. Give their back to God means… should mean… It is said, that my plan to bleed in Teofila's cranium came out of my thoughts and not through a vegetal twig of my chlorophyll dreams. That's what God says when I fall into the side of the colony, in the hemisphere of the found viceroys. Divine and human ignorance.

-I would have never imagined an ignorant God. The ignorant God should be ignored. How? Being a flower again.

-The sad little flowers —comments that suffered God that habits in churches and houses —cry when they hear the horrors perpetrated by my favorites, the humans.

-My family taught me how believe in God. Conscious God. Love God.

-I believe in that God. Dream…I have dreamt that the divine teeth have become stained with tartar, proper heavy smile, out of the heart of the jungle.

-Primitive God. Also ignorant….Could be that God… some God may be in favor of another specie. I won't deny that.

-Certain flowers- charged with venom and addiction —have made themselves enemies between the creator and human creatures. They wish to prove —these floral beings- that they are capable of assuming the sovereignty of the planet.

-And what does God think?

-But the lady flowers, assures the Green-God, damn, with time they'll get hands and legs, arms and head and teeth and you shall turn into sisters of man.

Great humorous answer. At least God has that indispensable sense.

I say in dreams to the hearty God:

-Let's go on one-way, Master, through one tunnel. From flower you can turn human, and from human to flower, from horse to ape and ape… Oh, I've become tired, yawn, tediousness is a sensation… goodbye, I'm going to sleep, Anselmo, do you hear?

-Yes, I hear.

At the wall on the back of the room there is an ivy presence.

-Now the image of deodorant talc for babies comes to my mind, which shows on its package the head of a child about to be devoured by a rose –I say with a deep voice, crow voice.

-I have seen that bottle. I have seen it. Pinky rosy face of a kid about to be covered by bloody petals. A devouring rose.

-I suppose that you have also dreamt such premonition. : we shall be eaten by the superior consciousness of the flowers. I imagine the art director during the process of its package design and say to myself: the image of the head about to be eaten by a rose must have come from subjective time. The mood of turning back to the gardens of Eden.

-My personal time, Mr. Storyteller. Time for a non-stop appetite. Time that... Someway, yes, the designing artist matches with... with my desire to abolish the work and effort.

-Three, four, thousand of times the publicist reproduced the image, but didn't dare to show it ferocious. Rose devouring baby, precious child.

-Cannibal flower.

-At the end, the roses shall be partners in crime with the poppies and marijuana, sisters of the wine and sugarcane liquor, cousins of peyote –fly back and forth to the back of the room. I realize that on the wall the geraniums have disappeared.

-If I would have chosen the path of the art director that designed the label, I would have put my own image on it, I am sure, premonition, back to the sleep, rest, and paradisiacal tranquility. I am leaving, I'm falling... goodbye. I never dreamt of a carnivorous rose.

-Tomorrow or the day after tomorrow, Anselmo, you shall keep on ignoring what in effect is to me indispensable to blurt out.

-That wish to ignore, look like God.

-You are a good listener, stay. Be careful, of course. I was going to tell you to close the doors just in case I would get in the mood to commit a murder. You find yourself outside and unguarded, I just started to get sleepier than you, and you shall be victim of easy punches. Fine, fall asleep, but man… not when he feels guilty, not when he has committed certain acts… not when he hates his girlfriend or sister, not when he's missed church two or three or twenty times on consecutive Sundays, no…

-I feel that my room and this site are the same space. Profane space and… primitive, mastered by the breath of the ignorant God. I have noticed that around my house azaleas grow in the corners. Suddenly a bush shines certain space in the house. There are also two bushes planted in the garden, two marijuana bushes.

-I am not a person to trust. Dishonesty revealed through meditation of deliriousness. The same alcohol prevents, positive vegetal message, hemisphere of love and not of hate, straight channel, do not drink, do not distillate, step away. Sugarcane and grapes at the service of the one who regrets: leave me, I am pernicious substance. I could be trusted once, Anselmo. I talk about the lapse that lasted since Teofila died until the time I lied naked on the bed of this ranch, by the way, somewhat hard and old, by the way, impregnated by death: somebody died here not long ago, isn't that right?

-Nobody that I know of. The room was filled with flowers to make more pleasant your arrival.

-Maybe your mother or your father passed away here, even though they weren't from this house but… I was going to say… I say that they were servants like you, inferior. The stench of death maintains itself alive, contradiction, a threat in a certain way, it invites one to disappear.

-It's not my own smell. I am complete away and apart. I… belong to a lower class. And fine with it. The hate…

-Interiority. That's what happens for interrupting my studies, for no haven been born to a rich family, for not being on the side of the dealers, I mean, dominated by the flowers –I move my black wings and see that on the back wall geraniums are starting to grow.

-I feel lied to. Frustrated. Only alcohol calms me, Mr. Storyteller. I don't feel like returning to the world of the sobers, for what? Human coherency is sick.

-There are a thousand lies that we ignore, Anselmo. I thought that I had forgotten Teofila.

-But you are, I want to think, I believe… descent person. I can tell from a distance that you are educated. Flowers don't receive any education, they are like I am, I identify myself with the humble simpleness of the flowers.

-I was. Sense taught at home, church child, once poster child. I was, during a long lapse of time I disguised myself as a good boy. I understand that in the past man covered himself with twigs our first fathers…

-Today's different. I dress a certain way and you… I am wishing that twigs grew on me, flourishing snow drops through the ears, long stems from the fingers.

-Gray suits. Black shoes. Conservative ties in red and gray tones. Dark socks. How serious. Now I know that I don't have to dress up as a bastard, instead the other way. You should know…

-I don't want to know. On the contrary. Ignore. Be on the side of the Green-God. Open mouth and let the daisies flow instead of words. I am tired of being.

-You should know, my friend, that the bones in the head crash and bleed, that our interior thought of any victim screams and insults, the murderer listen, what?, voice that says: you're against the specie, you're against yourself. Are you interested? Goodbye, dream with angels –back and forth from the wardrobe to the door, flying. Now the net of geraniums persists and covers the back wall.

-Send blessings and good wishes as if I was going to die. Only spirits waste time, lose space, confess any of their sins, since they want to confront God taking a certain degree of regret. My wife had already warned me: you well end up listening to what you shouldn't hear. I am standing in my own time, but somewhat interested to have my adventure between colonial bozos. You… Have you died of alcoholic congestion and are talking to a corpse? Am I going to die? Is my wife's life in danger?

-Not at all, Anselmo, I am sad to inform you that nobody ever dies. Die? It's about a dance, cosmos dance, cosmos choreography. It's about consciousness and different material. I am afraid that we are able to reproduce ourselves voluntarily. The traditional gestation is only one of the many ways to proliferate, one of the many ways that makes a specie dilate in space and time. The human birth is different to the birth of tortoises and the torturous birth. Species like all. Saints like San Francisco and Santa Teresa entered the dimension that I mentioned, THE US. Also the four evangelists: Juan, Marco, Matthew, Lucas. Plants and flowers are another being and in conjunction with animals. You'll see, I was born being who I am, but I can reinvent myself. As a matter of fact, I'm another one in the colony, completely human and completely animal, crow and man, man and crow. Filled with pains, remorse. We are sculpting artists, my friend. Just like the say: Architect of my own destiny.

-I don't understand a word you are saying about the conspiracy of the flowers, about the non-death... Maybe I do... One moment, I have taken out of my bag a pouch of rum and... I drank it all in one strong pull, opening my throat wide. The fermenting process was suggested by the flowers? I say... by the same grapes or sugarcane... green voices, macabre shining words, emerald color bounce in my cranium. I start to get the message, Mr. Storyteller,

little green bean stems... revelations of Dionises states.... That's how; by polite suggestion of the evil poppies we get morphine and heroine. That is how we can hit the skull of the girlfriend or whip with fury the Cross-of the Redeemer. Maybe –drunk- do you understand what I talk about, master. Maybe that's how you dream of the Mexican colony and know interesting people. You yourself were or are another human being and animal at romantic times? I must say that I have read it or read something about that man called Santiago Amendola, Is it about you? Well, the written comes to life. You are...I am...my grandmother taught me how to drink secretly. It is said with reason that alcohol gives bravery. Is it possible that the flowers start family feuds even wars? I am obsessed with the face of my wife. She... False and true bravery, I require her to continue listening to the confession. I confess that space starts to slide under my feet; I confess my will to fly. If I hadn't finished in the hands of the caretaker...I would have loved to be a priest. In times when Santiago Amendola lived, the storyteller, the priesthood had its importance, the saintly person was invited to dine, to give advices, to hand out divine punishments. For example, if some damned person hit a cross, hit him hard on the back. For example: punches and punishment to bread and water and to dress Sambenito.

Fry the hand of my wife… I have said to myself on may occasions that I should have accepted in a good way to belong to a group of slaughtering inquisitors. Two gangs: white and black. Something happens to my sense when I read about flagellations. I now declare that, to obtain major effect over punished parts, I would rub rough glove my beloved shoulder. From now I declare that I keep all kinds of whips. I now understand, that you can whip an ignorant God, the primitive God, green. Interesting. To continue to listen that I can escape through bottles of tequila that you hid in my wardrobe. Sober I can turn into a confessor, and give excellent advises. The moths don't drink. My grandmother would drink to stay in a good mood, through the bad deeds of my grandfather. Indifference to the humans through indigestion and stupefying. What do you have to say, Mr. Storyteller?

-I say while we are here dying or believing that we have died, my other selves are reproducing in our own times. Such superimposed personalities. Cards. Today we make up certain personalities and tomorrow another.

-Masks over masks. Shells. Have you thought, Anselmo, that we shade just like serpents do? The spirit is material. We model with it each thought. Every single act. The dog barks because it has barked and because it is happy to bark. Can a dog think? They actually think and talk. As a matter of fact they are entities –in their own dimension-, more important than us. Let's take the flowers and…Yesterday, reading a story about drugs… I fall into account that the flowers take revenge on the human aggressions creating spines and poisonous substances.

-We are the enemy. Well, and the primitive God, ignorant… We shall stop being enemies converting ourselves in branches, stems, and unconscious flora.

-Allow the complot of the flowers the non-stop proliferation the sale of stupefacient drugs. The soldiers of evil ease the return to paradise.

-God allows this absurd proliferation, against humanity and that is why it is necessary to punish him. On the other hand, I wish to continue thinking and on the other…

-The drug dealers don't know that they have been taken over by the superior mind of the flowers.

-But the ignorant God does know.

-They felt the conspiracy against the specie and convinced the drug lords to become their partners.

-I understand and approve that Santiago had a secret room and there... Jesus Christ had to bleed. Santiago the crow flew to the secret room and searched the whip with scorpions. Hit and denigrates with it, becomes less human.

-The flowers provide an addictive substance. Turn on the naïve humans and turn them back to Eden, lack of consciousness. Old and young junkies travel towards the region of flowers and are submitted to their minds painful madness. I have descended to that hell.

Me too, Mr. Storyteller, my wife...

-Down there I murdered my Teofila to take revenge on general Tejocote.

-Down there, I...

-Active pro-elitist. Whilst more drug addicts and dealers less aggression to the flora.

-Jesus Christ must bleed. We'll raise him on a cross. Punishing God going down the stairs that goes first through feathers, then through stems, inconsistent flora, you said it. I just expect that from the inconsistent active we may not surge again.

-The humans dead or crazed by the floral effects they shall reign in peace over the planet, next to the insects and other much less harmful animals –I see, from my place, the viceroy-crows sleeping on the wardrobe, that descends rings like a waterfall over the mirror.

-Could I talk with the viceroys that appeared? –asked Anselmo with a grassy tongue of drinks.

-Alcohol also comes from the vegetal kingdom. Grapes and sugarcane have come to an agreement. They hired Capone and a whole gang if American gangsters during the prohibition years.

-The ignorant God surged the prohibition because it consigned to finish mankind? The plants get closer to them through addictions.

-Of course yes and no –responded Anselmo with respect to the possibility of seeing my viceroys, crows sleeping on the wardrobe-. You see, the viceroys that appeared are no one else and mine. They are for myself. They are an integral part of my deliriousness.

-I could think they thou are inside my room to order my thoughts. I could suppose that, since I am also delirious.

-You can think it, Anselmo and you'd be correct. Let's talk on the phone with people that think they are opposite to us and that truly are mirrors of the true being. My multiplications.

-I talk here with rosebushes and lizards, Mr. Storyteller. On the wall run big fat lizards, family to the alligators and crocodiles. To them I have confessed my unpleasant being and wishes of drowning paradise. I can hear the noises of my brain. I ask and… The flowers respond to the call: come, Anselmo, let your feet grow roots.

-And our thoughts answer to the roses?

-They answer, suggest.

-You like me, Anselmo. I am sad. Terribly depressed. I am going to have to sleep a while. I shall spread the seeds out of myself. Plant them in the air…

-My wife shall give birth next Thursday, said the doctor. The veterinarian said that the hog of your cousin Ramon should have piglets soon. I don't know whether now is my opportunity. I don't know. Sleep always shall attract.

-I like this conversation through the door but I need to finish. Go to sleep the monkey wherever you can and I shall have to sleep here on the floor, whilst my viceroys continue in glares and forever useless explications.

By the way, Anselmo made offerings at home. Fruit, soup, tamales on the ground so his dead relatives could eat or dine.

-I have and keep the hope of my past… My grandmother comes down to sing suggestive and precise verses. I follow her while she dines and intones. That's is why… I can enter and see our viceroys before the geraniums grow too much on the walls, and the bugambilias.

-I haven't given to confess. I am doing it now because I am close –want to be- of the last sigh (am immortal. Shall live as a human or as a plant, as an animal. I change from one shape to the other, energy). Now I lighten my coat and despot because half between us the door. Door that separates my world from yours, Anselmo.

-With what objective did the viceroys appear to you? –asks Anselmo-. I thought about retiring to rest next to my wife, the lazy woman, but I shall not leave this place until I comprehend. I shall not go until I know if you or I am the invented one. Instead of staying asleep with my wife, it is necessary, next to your door.

I tap the door as a sign of agreement. A branch of bugambilia slides softly over the headboard of the bed. I look at it and it reacts becoming small because it feels that it has been seen in its intentions to invade everything.

The two viceroys, in reality were just one, inquire and inquired about the meaning of HEMOFICTION, Anselmo.

-Sense of mystery. Sense of immortality. Sense of sky and of hell. I shall stay. I shall not leave to the triviality when I have an opportunity to sustain a serious conversation with my life. That lazy woman can sleep on her own for once in her life. She can come and pick me up from the grass where I plan on sleeping shortly after understanding what cannot be, Mr. Storyteller.

-I hope that some differences and ideas that obsess me remain clear. For example, from all the women I have met, only Teofila keeps a privileged place.

-I knew Teofila with thick red lips. Under her skirt, she also had some beautiful lips, I mean, so well hidden that when she would show them I could actually feel that I had risen to the sky. My actual wife doesn't kiss well, with shame and too human. I love her tongue and she denies it to me. I love her pussy and she hides it between pajamas and the worst kind of underwear. Vulgar. What can make some in the world become irremediable?

I start to perceive the snores of Anselmo. He shall drool the door. In the best part of the conversation the string was lost and it throws itself upside down in the unconsciousness. To me it sounds convenient, because it talked about Teofila.

-I am not asleep, Mr. Storyteller. Just closing my eyes. I shall not get lost in your intimacy. You were talking about Teofila.

-I dream of her. I speak with her while I vigil. When I go to the canteen The Poor Peasant. The barman knows me there and so do the parishes. They know that I sit at the table next to the bathroom.

Did she die —that lady- of natural causes or forced?

-I understand that she shot my nature. Human bullet. Spiritual bullet. Especially after her death. Instead of eyebrows, she plucked moss from above my eyes.

-I wish we were all willing to confess. You have turned me into a priest. Tomorrow I shall have forgotten what you have said and shall think that I was hallucinating. In state of judgment you seem like an inoffensive individual.

-I am, Anselmo.

-Honestly, I don't doubt you. But Teofila's case…

-She died a longtime ago and has remained intact. My girlfriend never grew. Small girl. Very nice. She came to tell me that on earth I was not who I pretended to be. That I had a certain kinship with Jack the Ripper and other serial killers, cousins of flowers.

-Am I in danger?

-Nature.

-Did you know that you were going to kill?

-I understand that nature was conspiring in me before I met the girl –*crow nature, I peck on the floor and the wood of the door, while the viceroys-crow sleep. Plant nature. War inside of me with different toxic substances.*

-In me nothing conspires except a curiosity. I am curious by nature. I listen to things with an ill attention. The fights of my parents made me save a lot of money from going to the movies. Start from the beginning. I promise to keep on drinking and forget. I promise to enter delirium. Mr. Narrator, I die of boredom. Please, from the beginning.

-I can't jump the beginning and the same reason. I was also bored, I think.

-Teofila introduced herself.

-She kept absolutely live the instant that she greeted me. Hello, flower stuck in the left ear, clove. I was a well-behaved child back then. I liked to get good grades. Professor. Agustin Gonzalez would say that my intelligence would take me on extraordinary roads. It has been that way. I woke up, thanks to Teofila. Every day I step further away from the idea of a creator and enter the atheist coldness. It comes to my mind when I want to ignore the potency of the flowers calling to descend. The images sometimes want to talk tome. Saint Sebastian. Saint Bernard. Drop the drink and become human, they ask. Saint Joseph carpenter. Supposed father of Jesus. That last one opens the idea that I was the only boyfriend of Teofila. Teofila smiles at my internal pretensions. It isn't possible to see me three or four days, and become your lover forever. It is possible, Teofila, I swear. From the first moment I saw you… Ridiculous. She found it silly my absolute, round and definitive fondness to her.

-I have never loved that way. I have never been that passionate. Certain appreciation for the female accompanies my nights, yes… but I am tired, if my consciousness goes out…

The back of my room has grown. Shiny net of geraniums grows and fattens.

-The viceroys wish to talk, Anselmo.

-Let me listen

-I hate to think on clean and transcendental love. Unique encounters where doubt never appears —caws the albino viceroy, suddenly opening his eyes.

-The transcendent, the storyteller and Anselmo know it, strives on fixation, I mean, in the obsession. That is why you and I do not fit in the same body —affirms the black viceroy, giving feet around my bed.

-Because you are black. God imposed to finish our willingness to keep living unmercifully -the albino viceroy walked in the opposite direction of the black viceroy.

-Their voices of the viceroys sound familiar. Certain sadness comes to me to think of a separation of the viceroys inside our room. I would have preferred if two rosebushes would grow next to our bed and not human people.

-In history of separations comes always a superior willingness. I am talking again about god, gods, and spiritual dimensions. Forces of habit. Instead of observing with objectivity my case suddenly smears with metaphysical considerations that don't come to the sense. We talk about separations from white viceroy and black viceroy. We talk about nature. We talk about cells that get together with cells, complicated systems that culminate in beings that shine for days, months, years —my crow voice has be adjusted.

-I see the sky and stretch, especially when I'm drunk, when I understand that life is brief and mediocre.

-Flies and dragonflies. Dogs and cats form during a cellular progress. That seems so. I imagine that. From the sperm or seed planted in the female fountain the impossible starts to grow in front of one's eyes. I see what happens. I touch what I se that occurs. There's the phenomena in front. Teofila wasn't fiction. She knew how to express. She liked to go to school, carrying her books and pens in a blue bag.

-Before Teofila nobody had caught my attention –cawed the white viceroy.

And black one responded:

-Neither after. The case is that not even after. That's the mystery. I could have first found the beginning of love in that foreign body. But what I find… I find the impossibility of separation. I find her own nature in collision.

-I drink and cry. I drink and feel sorry. At the same time feel jealous. At the same time... Could you open the door and allow me to see the viceroys? –asks Anselmo-. Allow me to do so and afterwards turn into a flowerpot full of azaleas.

-I have cried. Cried thinking of my Teofila. I myself turn into two and sadden because I am not the only one. Cloning without hope of domination. The plates, addiction, have made me burst. You there and me here, Anselmo. Held face to face, reflection. Think much; by the way, it hasn't given me any results. I mean, it hasn't worked for... Instead of thinking that I keep myself in white looking at the walls in the living room, where nets of plants start to grow, climbing ivy. Peeled wall that explains nothing to me. It hasn't told me, for example, why did I have the parents that I had. Because my first girlfriend, named Teofila, decided to go with her parents to Guadalajara. You'll see, I said, Teofila, understand that I don't have anyone else. I understand, but I do count on them, with my progenitors, you should understand that it would be impossible for now, having only twelve years, staying next to you as if we were married.

-Before my sweet heart, who thinks about matrimony? I open my head and say to myself *sweet heart*, candy. I have gotten tired of the immense wish to feel united. For the millenary wish to become myself in two again. Anselmo and my Teofila, the girl that I haven't found. I understand what you say, Mr. Storyteller, because I have remained always outside. A door that keeps me separated from what kills my curiosity. Have I always been the same man? I doubt it. I doubt it because as a worm it moves inside me and I say to myself: you were another more complete one in another galaxy, in another dimension, in some universal movement. God or the devil has split me into two. Provoked in me this nostalgic separation. One could that I am in hell. One could suppose that hell is not earth and the separation, precisely. I am now suffering my curiosity being outside the case. I hear outside. Hear the cold of the grass even though I get warm with the drinks. Soon I shall throw up rosebushes. Soon my lazy wife shall start to call me: old man, old man, your dinner is ready. I shall sit at the table crying. Really, woman, you'll see, I was talking to the storyteller, cousin of our boss Mr. Ramon, and I felt something missing. I felt that I needed something more. Double condition of the being. Double headed. Double thoughts that in reality unites itself to one. Un prehistoric times we were male and female, I know. What did you say to the dead girl who was your sweet heart?

-What did I say to her? You can stay in my body inside. We can be two in one. Fake hermaphrodite.

-I am deeply saddened. I know that that absence –when it presents itself –fills an empty jar. Fills it immensely with the own soul. Half worm. That's what I need. I had or used to have two heads, Mr. Storyteller, maybe I had wings on my back and lost them. When I turned eight, I asked for my birthday what I needed. What? –asked my parents- The other thing that I needed, was another sex integrated to myself, *sweet heart.*

-My girlfriend Teofila never understood what I meant until she was hit by the hammer. Nailed. I felt like a carpenter like the father of Jesus. Teofila's death was like building an own casket. One buys the nails oneself. One buys the wood and hammer oneself. If you were not in me, I would say to myself, you're in distance. Out of myself. In the dimension of Nostalgia. Where is interned by plenty meditations. Where past times appear. To perform Teofila's death was indispensable. With that deed came my morn. What I am suffering now. I said to myself then –being stuck to the death that I myself built: you are not the only murderer. Green-God separated us. Viceroys and listeners have killed all along history. Neron burned Rome. Next, I wetted my address book with blood. Kissed her forehead and paleness. Ran to the bathroom and stood up straight so the water from the shower would wash off my past. I cleaned every single suspicious stain and decided to disappear forever. That carpenter hasn't come back and has decided to change profession. Until now, lying naked on this bed in the ranch of my cousin Ramon nobody has related my hands with the death of that girl. On the contrary. I assisted to her burial. I cried with absolute sincerity. General Tejocote cried. Fifteen years have passed. Impugn crime, like many others. Then I understood and said to myself: I shall never be a good boyfriend. I shall never be a grateful person in society because I am missing my other half.

-I am drunk, my eyes wish to close, but continue, please, I die of curiosity. Before being two we were hydrangea, moss, lilies and orchids.

-We continue with the story of the viceroys split in two. It seems to my person. They look like the two viceroys that in reality are one to the boyfriend of Teofila. They try to explain, during the tendency of HEMOFICTION which occurs in me and because I feel lonely. Green-God, primitive, it split us. To be two instead of one. Divisions. Conflictive. Neurosis.

-That's what I need to hear. That I am just I alone. My own half since I have been thrown into paradise by the fury of divine punishment. As I child I thought that taking communion would complete myself, but no. The emptiness continues which is now filled with alcohol, nice substitute.

-Now I touch the real problem. Loneliness. I was about to say infinity. Infinite loneliness. Was tempted, but understood that this loneliness doesn't touch the beyond. It'll not take over time. I expect. It's about something –enormous sensation- from this world. Were two, thousands of years ago and before… vegetal fever. The body of the viceroy became two. Instead of one boyfriend, Teofila has now two. Treading the present and the past at the same time. United moments. Attached times between themselves. Where are we? Here. Now. Room of the ranch of Ramon. Golden bed. I have been thinking about committing suicide but am regretting it. I need to finish my memoirs. I am talking about Teofila. About Teofila's death. Emotional space and time. Comprehension. Millenary absence, nostalgic from the other, you and I. I am a pot about to explode, Mr. Anselmo. That's why my friends and my actual wife, Canuta, said to me: go and get well at the ranch. You'll think over there. Here I am, watching the viceroys. I must make clear that since Teofila's death, I haven't committed a single mistake. What mistake did God commit by separating us? The same one as I did. I have been a perfect nobody. I remember that I said to myself something similar looking at the corpse of the girl: It hasn't descended from the sky, the angel that announced Christ's arrival. And I expected an angel. That one. As a matter of fact, my evil deed provoked. As a matter of fact my deed must have made noise in the heavens if a heaven exists… Dada. The blood of Teofila wet the tiles on the floor. Nothing. Fifteen years after splitting into two, I feel an absolute necessity to keep myself in the ranch and release the viceroys that wish to explain. They say, that in a certain way, the crime doesn't allow me to become two, sexually speaking. Now I am two and even three but only in one way. Only man, going through nostalgia and sadness because I need my sweet heart, I killed her, or the one that Green-God murdered before, millions of years before.

Large bugambilia branches have come through that almost half of the room. I pinch the windowsill. Smells of floral freshness.

Let's go back to the viceroys: silent and fast separation that left a bitter taste on the tongue and certain dizziness. The viceroys look at each other. Mirror. If it was about a new birth, the viceroys would have been crying after the invisible doctor would have slapped them on their buttocks. I was born to know my girlfriend. I was born to unknow my parents and my parents I. I say that I was born to unstick and end up stuck as a lonely person. Teofila my girlfriend –first love- persist yet in silence. Different silence to the one that the mandatories found. This silence –the other- hurts. That empty silence is filled with panic. It has a sign on it saying: this person is gone forever. I left myself through it. A girl of only twelve years of age. Blond hair. Honey. Silence, they are men that were just born and take reality as adults, no complaints, only confusion –and cawing I go back and forth from the bed to the back of the room.

The viceroys talk. They talk to me. They say to the crow that rests on the pillow:

-Hello.

-Hello.

-Where did you come from?

-From you.

-I didn't know Teofila, your sweet heart,

-She was the first love of the storyteller –the black viceroy looked at himself in the mirror of the wardrobe with a certain neurotic insistence-. Naked man. Crow. Now macho. Man that has kept quiet for many years and more years and suddenly wants to burst. They say that the killers die to confess. It seems like the present case confirms it all. Storyteller wishes to talk and understand. That's why he has called us. He thinks that we know Jack the Ripper. He thinks that he can fool us. When he gets tired he shall go back –thinks- to the house of his wife Canuta to continue a life full of nothing, full of sassy Christmases, and birthdays with unimportant gifts. Outside Anselmo awaits him asleep. He can't hear anymore. He has drunk too much. Thrown up on the door. Congestion. We see that Anselmo has branches grown on to him that substitute his feet, roots.

It was she. She was there. She suddenly stopped being here. My loneliness became deep. The prior loneliness, which was already big, became fatter in such a way after she announced her departure. I am going to Guadalajara. I am leaving with my parents. She sure had the others, not I. I was born to unstick.

Anselmo's roots, his feet, sink into the wet ground. Tomorrow I shall see him flourishing on the other side of the door.

Exit door to the door had squeaked. I say, during the separation of the viceroys, white and black. Silence. Dog outside of dog has barked. The viceroys-crow not. That yes, both individuals, born of the same matter and spirit saw the separation experimenting cramps on the left toe. I lived it with them. Simultaneous cramps on three toes which in reality are just one trying to explain, trying not to convert in some hard branch, vegetal extremity. If there is no God in the sky –because there isn't a sky either- only myself in loneliness. I am the unstuck, except for the absence-presence of Teofila. Others like me –murderers, let's say- can offer certain clues of comprehension. I wasn't made. That's how I came out. Then, I wish to penetrate in my nature. That's how I came out. Why? What does "came out" mean? Did the viceroys also come out trying to explain to me the impossibility of a hermaphrodite transformation? Soon they recovered from the stitches on the toe standing puzzled in front of each other, somewhat nervous, with the mouths open of astonishment. It is surprising to be that way. Precisely like that and no other way. Instead of Dad or Mom, first words of any newly born, the white viceroy wanted to use the gift of speech to inquire immediately about the sense of HEMOFICTION, because it raised him doubt and confusion. His twin, also showed himself intrigued, responding with relief.

-Two. You and I. Both male but not found in another sense. Different to the sexual sense.

-You, I and the storyteller.

-And Mr. Anselmo, lying outside.

-Storyteller. The person who shall be explained.

-The person that wishes to fill with lights his loneliness.

-Phrases. The light is empty. The light does not fill.

-Talks about good actions.

-Most of his deeds have been bad.

-If I were he, I'd seek for the light of forgiveness. To cry is good. Regret.

-Good for what?

-When your purpose is to live in peace. Teofila is in peace now.

-I doubt it. Allow me to doubt it. Teofila shakens. Her spirit.

-You are going to wake up Anselmo.

I fly and peck on the window, from where I can see Anselmo's feet, every time with more roots that deepen the roads to paradise.

Separation. Two viceroys. Loneliness. Two flags in a life and in the government. Left and right.

-Two wholes.

-Two lonely wholes. Nostalgic wholes because they need their sweet heart.

Both miss the presence of Teofila. But if it that presence existed, they'd still miss it. I explain: Teofila would be missed and even if she were here she'd be missed. That's at least what I have understood. Teofila can't fill me and nevertheless I'm sure that she can.

-Unstick from me, Mr. Storyteller -asks the girl from my memoir.

-Tell me how.

-You have understood that I am not the cause of your emptiness. Green-God separated us.

-I have understood that. The emptiness always refers to you.

-The hammer hurt.

-I don't remember that moment. I see myself cleaning. Unsticking the accusing blood. After that I see myself leaving to the conservatory. In solfeggio class. In guitar lessons. The teachers say: bright boy, plays Bach and Villalobos well. I don't say a thing. I smile. I will not dedicate myself to music. Why? Because I need Teofila. Because I'm not going to tell them what I need. I left the Conservatory and was taking drawing lessons. My teacher made me copy flowerpots and pumpkins.

-You copy well.

-No matter what, I'm not satisfied.

-That seems good -says the teacher looking at me with delight.

-I would like to copy your thighs and belly, miss. May I?

-If you are only going to look at them… sure… will you.

-I will have to get closer. A lot. I will have to taste you, may be. I wish to taste the air that blows close to your sex.

-We're in the hall. Let's step into the room.

-Let's go to the garage.

I work as a crow on the floor of my room. I see that Anselmo's head is full of little flowers.

Contrary hemispheres facing each other, under the moonlight –the eyes are already used to the dueling and revise, throwing shines of intelligence. Time has gone back. Tantrum. I don't like what exists and is tailless. Now I live another life of loneliness in the past. I walk to my house on the bridge… I talk with myself and with an animal. Teofila's soul. Soul of my necessity to become complete. Soul of absence. My diary shall register this retraction of natural mode because it was a natural fact. From the ranch of my cousin Ramon I went to the colony. Empty. Always the emptiness guides me. I come and go. Walk. Stay or go is the same to me if she's not with me. Depression. One sees that the walls in the hose deteriorate. One sees that the shower stings and disappears. Meaning: that time has gone back to its own, thanks to my depression. I travel when I feel depressed. When I feel guilty of hitting the girl with the hammer. Teofila had decided –decision, you may have noticed that I repeat the words with irony –to remain in the Conservatory until I become I pianist. I was playing at the time of her death the first piano and solfeggio. IU go out to walk as I remember Teofila sitting giving useless scales –uselessness also repeats itself in my diary because it causes my mood falls. Useless is synonym of laziness. Synonym of equality. Everything is the same to me. Steps over the bridge. I wish to cross myself and I do it, mechanically. I am not catholic but I have to be so in front of the ones who can see me.. Look, I say, look at me; I am drawing a cross on myself. Damned hypocrites. You call me a demon. Am I? Not at all. I talk with the crow. The creature crazes whoever don't know it. The neighbors think that they'd rather have me leave the house together with a dog. Why? More animal than a dog… I have left behind my old personality. Step the past.

On the railing of the bridge cawed a crow that was a person. It is not known whether he went from being an animal to person or vice versa. The neighbors mentioned large colloquies in the rooms of the house between crow and being human, outbursts of bad words, laughter and mimes. Crow and person loved themselves as if they were one.

Crow and person woke feelings of fear, repugnancy and curiosity. I talk of person –myself in third person because a feel foreign to myself. See that the nosey neighbors find it strange that somebody lives and talks with animals. It could happen to a widow that has dogs. The men shouldn't live alone and even less live with a repulsive crow. Of course, the viceroys have followed me to this new home in time. But they have not forgotten about Anselmo lying outside the door of my room in the ranch of Ramon. They constantly tell me:

-I am one.

-I am also one.

I talk in the present. I haven't been able to leave this world. I am still here searching for Teofila. Times found. Tomorrow is past and vice versa. I carry with me the obsession. The crime. If I could shut it up for fifteen years…I would think that general Tejocote deserved what happened. It seems to me that in exchange to what had happened, not to the mother of the girl. She held eternal mourning. She held a constant cry. Cries of **Llorona**. Oh, my Teofila! Oh! -she cries out to the four winds and I in disgrace hear her no matter how dirty my ears are.

-Ma'am, why do you cry after so many years and now we find ourselves in another era.

-Oh! Oh my Teofila!

-To flee wasn't that easy. My dad warned me: Son, always go on the right side of the road, you shall avoid wasting your time, waste of eras, waste of dawns and more dawns of sun and moon. Maybe at the moment that he gave me the warning… I am tempted to put once again the decisive word. I decided to become a Christ on earth. I walked with that decision to Teofila's house and whack! I hit her with the hammer. Green-Christ. Separating. Forgive that I repeat this one scene, which remains in my mind, which wakes me up without caring how drunk I go to bed. The anger wakes me up sometimes. I get up and throw pots in the kitchen against the wall. I throw apples and food that stick to unimaginable places. At my age people turn moody. My character has actually changed. I am older and live with fewer commodities. Stuck to the gruesome memory of Teofila.

One plus one is two in one –caws the black viceroy.

-Man of the king –caws the white.

-Minor agent before the majors and majors before minors.

At times I feel that the talk of the viceroys seems like the one of the crow. Between both they make one. Between both the copy the say of the spoilt animal. Teofila decided –underline- to become a pianist. She opened the latch of the new piano that the general had taken to her on one of his visits at home. Go, my dear, the man said to the girl, I have brought you the most expensive piano in the store.

The vertical piano that sounds much better because it costs much more.

-The important thing is that it sounds, daddy. He's going to give me the company that you deny for being in the army –in true life, to his big house, where he also had daughter, two young ladies eighteen and twenty-one who are ready to get married. It was very noticeable that Teofila was illegitimate.

Anselmo moves outside without waking up. The growth of herbs on his belly is what makes him move.

-You came out of me –caws the albino crow.

-And you from me -caws the black.

Teofila in the past, time where my friend Anselmo sleeps. Where I hope –maybe not anymore- I can tell him the rest of the story. It is not strange to hear in these places the snores out of era, his snores are out of place. That is a ranch, Anselmo, please; I have traveled to colonial times. Religion has its importance. Moral roughens. Here and there Christians are seen and solemn Christians. Beings that are afraid of the night because of Ghosts, because of Vampires. My age is not the same anymore. Nevertheless, I continue remembering the conversation that we had through the door for the first time that the viceroys appeared.

-White cross embroided on the cape –cawed the white viceroy.

-Black cross –cawed the black.

The mandataries fly towards Anselmo and, transformed into humans, they cover him from the cold. The man trembles in early season. The man gets consumed. I can die of congestion. His wife, the lazy one has cried: come back, you damned animal, come Anselmo, come here and I'll pull out your moustache. The cries of the lady haven't reached the ears of the conscious Anselmo. They have entered his sleeping ears to build a strange nightmare. Anselmo lives with her the idea of a person divided in two viceroys and a storyteller. Divided in two different times. The one of Teofila as a person and the one of Teofila as an animal. Girl turned into crow. Crow full of rage for having died without concluding its studies in the Conservatory.

The mouth of Anselmo opens and shows the green stem instead of a tongue.

-Religion upside down –says the white viceroy while he drinks a beer-. We practice it in silence us the viceroys but straight. I pray how God commands. I behave at the market how God commands. Of course, I am out of Anselmo's time, but not in the actual. Here, on the contrary, I feel well walking dressed as I am. Talk about religion and about saint stamps. The lady with the belly that sells tamales at the corner of the cathedral says that she likes me a lot. The same affirms the rich lady that goes to mass every evening at seven. This sane person talks with the priests. Underneath, she passes the money happily. Let's avoid talking about Jack the Ripper and the horrendous crimes committed by the storyteller –now it flies towards outside of the room, and poses on the shoulder of Anselmo.

-On the contrary, standing up –responds the black viceroy, just recovering its human form-. Standing religion. I draw a crow without believing. Damn, it's about living life and nothing else, I say to myself, after leaving the confessionary. Always feeling like throwing a tremendous insult in the middle of mass, tremendous blasphemy that makes the saints template. The storyteller has given his part of his personality to mine. The storyteller hasn't forgotten the crime and dares to step in church without feelings. It is not possible to enter the temple of God carrying such horror in the stomach. Let's go out to rest on the bridge and after the bridge fly back home.

The three crows, we fly and put the claws on railing of the bridge, cawing: "Hemofiction, Hemofiction".

Anselmo is removed from his site by the growing of the green stems.

Many priests and friar exist in the present as in the past –*my crow eyes have seen it in temples and monasteries.* Many Indians and crossbreds in search of a place –*social collocation based un unreal dreams.* It's about being in society. It tries to be useful. I am not that way and am not trying to be so. I act like the plants, without shame. I am nobody and not trying to be so. The careers that others do bore me. Jackass, Jackass, my father would call me if he could. Here in this new present, the only thing that exists is my house, the neighbors, crows, the viceroys and solemn size –*it weighs like a cape thrown black shadow especially what surrounds me.* There where Anselmo is lying, some would be happy to return to the unbearable hypocrisy. Whoever talks against the church is immediately accused and taken to the Casa Chata to receive torture. There's a so-called Mr. Ferrara that cries in the house in front of mine because I'm his neighbor. Because he is saying that I have a pact with the devil. Nothing like that, Mr. Ferrara, the devil doesn't exist, neither does God, but a great big mouth that wishes to devour us does.

We are three crows chatting on the railing of the bridge. – Spanish. Creole. Crossbred –says the albino crow-. During this time I experimented rejection on part of the three. The Spanish rejects me because of envy of position that I didn't have, since I am a viceroy in hallucination, fake viceroy. Creole sees me from down to up, also envying who I am. Crossbred the same. Owner of a barbershop o a service car. Beyond money is the condition. I am a noble person and a rich crossbred can't be one no matter what. As a viceroy I have introduced myself in some kind of a laundry of a friend in an area of the less fortunate, and the women would go crazy: my love, Mr. Viceroy, I want a child with you and more –in choir all the gossip women. I ask you all to show me your asses and they gladly do, begging his highness not to tell anything to their husbands the swings they have with me.

-Black, damned, stay in the air and respond black viceroy crow-. Adjectives don't touch me. On the thigh of the damned the word signs reality. Reality is the same as a word. That poor is damned. That poor is black. That poor came out white but was born in Mexico, not in Spain. We are two viceroys out of nowhere. Two people that unite and wish to argue to reach an unreal agreement –positive and negative, heads or tails on the coin falling in dual direction and synchronizing each face, nullifying the sense of luck.

-I was born by luck.

-Your mother is my mother.

Anselmo snores, still making noise, although he has almost turned into a tree.

I peck on the windowsill. The viceroys look at me. Flesh and bone, it's the same unfolded and dressed in opposite and repelling colors. Now I wish to suppose that they were born with Anselmo's drunkenness, lying on the door of the ranch. Now I wish to blame for my opening and astral trips to that man that I barely know. Could I grade astrology to theses sudden changes of era? But, why would these viceroys come out of Anselmo and not out of me? As a matter of fact, the unfolding happened in my room, although it was in the ranch of my cousin Ramon. And in the ranch the constant drunkenness of Anselmo rules. I know because the man showed himself. Knocked on my door and immediately pulled out a small bottle of rum. One first and then another. An then a bottle of tequila that I handed out. I wanted to hear about Teofila because the individual felt nostalgic. He knows about the other part that most humans are missing. At least some of them. My person and his. Teofila appeared to show off and understood the mistake, but didn't refer to the murder, maybe because of him, a time ago, he hammered a brain and immediately buried it. Duration. Anselmo sleeps outside of the room in another time. There he returns to paradise, which is any drug addicts friend of the flowers dream. Dream that I am myself. Dreams that the viceroys belong to him. Dreams that Teofila was killed because she was hit with a hammer. Damn mental crisis. Damn madness. If somebody leaves even for two seconds of the usual coherency, thousand of accusations come to mind. You are not a corded man, Anselmo would say to himself and I would repeat at my same contagiousness. I shall have to rebuild what I am blamed for in another way: I see Anselmo meeting Teofila. Teofila says to him: I love you, Anselmo, I love you for all my life. Then I hit. With the hammer I separate my love from the love of Teofila and dirtied myself. Anselmo hadn't appeared when you said that your parents were taking you to Guadalajara.

-Anselmo was boyfriend before I even knew you, but I thought it was all right for you to love me too, Mr. Storyteller; that you would love me like the girl that I was and not as a wife for the rest of life. I wasn't prepared. I wished that my dad would stay more days with us at home. I wished to walk held by his hand on

Saturdays and Sundays. That he would hurry me in the mornings so I wouldn't be late at the Conservatory. My dad –a general. I saw him as the biggest man on earth, the most tender and kind man. I never understood why he chose to go with the army. I said to him: Dad, the army isn't a person; the army can't touch you with my hands.

-Me white –cawed the albino crow.

-Me black.

Branches grow out of Anselmo's ears.

I see the viceroys with crow's eyes. Same nose. Same tongue. Black styles under ones neck and white in the other. Same cape and ties. Black horse and white horse tied to the same tree outside, close to where Anselmo sleeps his last human dream.

-What the hell is HEMOFICTION? –he asked.

The viceroys caw. Teofila wishes to intervene and tell her version of the facts. Wishes to explain with childish words what hemofiction means.

-Yes, what is what? –asks the girl in my mind.

-Genre or stream sister of horror –responds the black viceroy imitating the voice of a friendly and loving person, pressed tone, voice that doesn't correspond., sunken tone in a role that results too tight and slimy, zombie acting a false jubilee for having been buried alive –I am happy who I am, thinking as most Christians-Catholics think, most middle class people, Franciscan and Jesuit presentation with the touches of a letter or inquisitor –I am an educated being, worthy to be admired, my accumulations of facts go through my tongue with a certain search causing admiration-. HEMOFICTION runs parallel to horror in multiple and morbid interests, but it separates in aspects of form and content, you see –the black viceroy has taken of his hat to scratch his bald and shiny head. Such greasy baldness creates the idea to slide and comb the nonexistent. His twin also scratches himself. It is possible that the viceroy double has picked up lice, there are many in the castle. It is possible that his shaving may have reached strong parts. The same blade that scraped the pubic hair without mercy, going to the back with anger to finish the itchy pest.

-Explain to me, please, with simple words –asks Teofila in my mind.

Anselmo has stopped snoring. His body stands up and stays in front of the door, next to the other tree.

Anselmo doesn't scratch himself nor drool lying next to the door of my room. He doesn't understand anymore. Impossibility. We humans sign and name. Adam and Eve did it. Here is suddenly this winged and fat worm. Here we see a black butterfly. Over there twists a hairy serpent. We study its behavior. Curiosity. Tree of good and evil. The word understanding for the scientist is just born which he pronounces disappearing before his eyes the reality which has just been classified. That worm isn't the same one anymore. It has jumped from the time of the first one to the time of the second.

Caw on the bridge. The viceroys caw posing on Anselmo's arm, which has almost become a branch.

From the interior of my viceroy's hat jumps a toad saying *I am father and have eaten my tadpole. I am lover and have eaten the lady of my dreams, delicate and submissive, allowed her to stare dark and flirtatious winks close to the floor. Dad once chased me in. I could get away from his fangs hiding inside the magical hat.*

I respond as a crow to the toad just emerged from the hat:

-My name is Santiago and I came from that hat. I am person and crow. Santiago Amendola and not Teofila. I got floral addiction to return like Anselmo to vegetal unconsciousness. Because of Nostalgia. Green-God separated Teofila from me. I came out of that hat. Then the hat exists. Exists in my house and the Christ found by the nosey *–thrown and spit.* Three family members from the inquisition allowed to register and hit the door of the house with a large stick. Demolish and enter my room. They and some other neighbors armed with crosses and missals. Dressed in bright black. Sequences and silver string. Their elegance shall accuse. Accuse the immaculate decency *–perfection only sustains through addiction, triumph of the flowers over the church and government.*

Let's put the scene in present: Neighbors and family in the secret room of my house and discover my absence cawing next to black feathers, a bleeding Christ and diverse instruments of torture. They said, with reason, that in reality I was a person and crow at the same time *–and next a plant.* They said, with reason, that I would talk to myself when I dialogued with the crow –myself- who calls himself Santiago and not Teofila. Missing. I am the half of myself although I am animal and human person. I am two machos when I should have become two, masculine and feminine. My story of drunkenness and witchcraft exists. Green-God wants me back. I shall become once again hermaphrodite and immediately after and plant or bush. I live in an elegant house, always surrounded of men that like to get drunk and high, and bare the pestilence that comes from my body and clothing. I could call myself Anselmo and be lying outside of the door of the room of the storyteller, but…I could be that is not me, but… I could complete the presence of somebody, but… I myself feel empty, except when I lock myself up in the secret chamber *–hits and punches against the Green-God that separated* *me from Teofila.* Inside there, practicing my loves, filled of boos for instants –*kicks and punches.* Suddenly my person swells becoming two. As if they were two saint crows art the same time. What greatness, misters. What scandalous satisfaction –*when I hit a spit the Green-God.*

-I feel like God Almighty, God the magnificent, magician wrapped in a long black and red cape, with a red cross embroidered on my back. Andersen made me up during a painful reign. I am absent person. Let the caulderon in and out again. Lived in pits and mouse holes. Anselmo knows me, I mean, knew me. As a child we played together in the puddles, next to the pit in the ranch. Sometime he took me to school and I learnt how to read. My studies were interrupted because the teacher, Miss Teofila, discovered my presence inside of Anselmo's right pocket. Sneaky boy, damned child, yelled Miss Teofila, pulling the hairs of that child. Furious then, Anselmo threw me in the teacher's face. Miss Teofila fell on her back on the grass. From her split mouth and cranium to long red streams of smelly blood started to flow. I said to death: I am not a hammer, ma'am, and your grace should have been a pianist and not a teacher. That is the frustration that made you burst.

I peck on the windowsill, next to the toad. The viceroys caw on top of the wardrobe.

They would have eggs for breakfast and part of the yellow would spill over suck or shell. I would eat mole and part would remain smeared on my face, hair and hat also on the clothing which I already mentioned before. Capes of tastes covered capes of taste. Of course that I was pointed at, when I went to the market or when I sat at the balcony to talk with myself in the form of a crow. The averted blood today by the Christ in suffering sums today. Double food, two different classes, spiritual and material *–flora requires it that way, it was foreseen that way, human investment, retrocede towards the paradise earth.*

The toad answers, without moving, with a rough voice:

-The clothes that the crow doesn't carry still smells. If he moves it smells of rotten blood, beans and noodle soup, grilled meat and **chiles rellenos.**

-I have never seen a toad like you. I hope that the prince that you carry inside is handsome. You have good teeth.

Rarely are seen animals of the specie in New Spain, blessed with teeth as sharp and big as mine. The creature seems about to go through metamorphism to a bat, if it should get wings, of course. Of so many times entering and exiting the hat it will turn out mutating. Will your being be contagious?

-You don't understand a thing –specified the toad.

-Nothing –confirm the viceroys –crows, after cawing.

The roots of Anselmo are supporting the tree. It shall soon become heavy and eternal.

The crow which was I would tell me mysteries to the ear, so beautiful that I forgot to take a bath; so beautiful that I didn't care what animal would spoil or damage the house and the secret room where the cries of Christ remained locked in suffering. Little by little, in a matter of time, it's beak started to peck the furniture and curtains –and the sensitive nerves of Christ. Savage herb started to grow on the corners of the house. The crow never received a threat from me. I don't threaten myself; on the contrary, I caress myself alone. Maybe the toad confirms my story, but I see that it doesn't care.

-I come from an invisible pond. I jump the same in the halls of government that in Casa Chata of the Inquisition –replies the toad with dignity-. Adore the houses in ruins that allow the growth of green and threatening beings.

-Normal toads are gross, but even worse are the ones that come out of magnificent fountains.

-There was once a toad that at night would grow as a hydrangea.

-People would come home, but I never had friends, just myself, as a say, auto sufficient person and crow. My feathers love my feathers.

-Is it about reality or fantasy? –the white viceroy hits the toad, but it doesn't manage to scare him away too much and the animal falls on its feet making a blunt and loose sound. Body and sound unite in one unsteady truth, full of vibrations that attract old echoes of primogenitors. Croak and pose on the left shoulder of the white viceroy, saying:

-At my house, there is no more room than for myself. Bugambilia branches under the roof, come through the cracks.

-I am hungry. Old and desperate hunger. Indian and Creole hunger, crossbred and black.

-Who eats and doesn't spill lacks of nature. Who sweats and washes, lacks of nature. Why shouldn't our feet stink? The neighbors would call me Perfumed Santiago. Lions stink. Why should man be clean?

-The toad jumps from shoe to shoe of the white viceroy.

What does a cannibal toad and a human crow have to do in a white and decent vice regal story? –asked the albino viceroy, drumming the fingers on the window sill, from where Anselmo's growth can be observed. It seems as if it'll be a jacaranda.

-They're united –from crow and toad- the wish to slide again as a plant, chlorophyll consciousness. Tomorrow she shall grow like a bugambilia, without thinking.

-The black viceroy caws on top of the wardrobe. He shall return to the vegetal, I forecast it. While you smoke more pot, my son. While you drink more alcohol, son.

-My toad son tasted like a toad –like a frog. The little toad tasted like a frog and the frog that was my lover like a toad, by the way very tender and friendly, prayed the rosary every afternoon, maybe with hope that I would stop drooling when I watched her –the carnivorous toad looks at the white viceroy with hunger.

-*Its teeth kissed me and so did its stomach* said my frog - affirms the carnivorous toad, preparing to jump.

It's holds back its jump when I say:

-I think about the grease on my wings and not about toads eating toads. Only a few storywriters: Hoffmann, Perrault, Andersen y of course Swift would allow themselves such grotesque scenes –father toad devouring son toad and lover frog- because their minds –toy clockwork- sweat infant cruelty and archaic, witches well and ogres. Before... or after the carnivorous ferocity the vegetarian peace awaits, not to be human, goodbye arms and eyes and comeback green blindness, goodbye head and ears.

-And the little toad humped his lover as they fornicated. After he sat to cry on half of the staircase and asked Toad God to return his lover because he missed the kisses and bites.

-What relation is there between horror and the table? –asked the white viceroy, offering to the crow to peck a biscuit crumb off his shoulder.

Direct relation between carnivorous ferocity and horror is all –affirms the toad. The plants are peaceful, but we do miss being like Anselmo, lying turning into a Jacaranda. I like to talk about food and females and castles where curiosity opens its mouth to extreme crimes –the look of the carnivorous toad has become dark and evil-. It's not that bad to die between loving teeth –said my frog before I bit her.

    -Perfectly white love the vegetal –said the milky viceroy.

No matter how much the white viceroy tries to avoid it, imagines the toad biting to bits the little toad and the lover with appetite, similar meat with a taste that reveals his own.

-I shall become vegetarian –assures the milky viceroy, throwing up.

-The toad croaks, putting on his head small black hat.

-I ate in love –*emotional ecstasy tied with pleasure*. Loved the little boy, my son, and the silent and serene lady.

-I feel tied to the world through the food and its smells. Every time red blood from the risen sprays on me, I get feelings to touch –I say and peck the windowsill, feeling guilty.

-Internal pulsing took me to eat what I liked the most –affirmed the toad, jumping on the floor. Looking for the left shoe of the albino viceroy.

- Congenital psychotic disposition –diagnoses the viceroy dressed in white-. Gnome that guides homicides, evils and perverts –shake the toad, but it is too stuck to its foot-. Regression, the vegetarian soldiers feel nostalgia of its origin and wish to return. So we shall return to Eden gladly, garden where Green-God reigns.

The black viceroy intervenes:

-I am attracted to sex that eats sex with the eyes. Sex that hurts. The sick with a congenital psychotic disposition adore, like Sade, a God whose essence is evil. Logically, the evil impulses deviates the superior compulsive evil. And there is nothing superior to the wish of return towards the green world, attraction, why walk if one can drag? Why talk if one could be white in plain paradise?

-D.H Lawrence concentrated the same illness on the idea of nature. To God Father, said, we find him in flesh.

-Thanks to it Swift composed his Modest Proposal –the black viceroy points out, imitating the movements of his equal.

-And Edgar Poe his Bernice -the toad jumps from foot to foot of the white viceroy.

-And Jack the Ripper his Gut Poems .the black viceroy transforms into a crow and flies around the room.

I say, suddenly turning into Santiago Amendola.

-It is talked about the poles in love. Penis and vagina. My negative pole was in the secret room, where it expelled my animal and vegetal anxieties. God is the evil because it impulses to treat him bad *–evil is the voice of the plants, the mouth of an immense jungle.* Green-God wishes that we return to start or begin from the plants. I ignore that that stage stopped in my development –animal and human growth. I don't know when nor why I felt the impulse to hit and torture the Christ that was hidden in my secret room –puberty of the human and the crow. The same impulse made me murder Teofila. Simply locked myself in with the saint and became addicted to drink his blood and sighs *–I go back as a crab, feel like putting roots like Anselmo. Get away from Teofila's crime.* During the day I felt a certain illness that I tried to calm by eating fruit and vegetables. Nothing. I went with my key then and opened a secret door. Hard against the wooden flesh of the Messiah, hard with whips, spikes and spit, hard with the hammer and nails to reach the ecstasy that keeps me jailed. Prison that goes from man to crow and vice versa. Dungeon of torture to orgasm. Jail from the animal to the plant. Now I know that an arm –branch- gigantic one has been calling me for quite some time before the birth of the animals.

-Maybe some psychiatrist reads jungle in my brain, floral mouth, open to abysm -Comments the toad, returning to leap from foot to foot of the white viceroy.

I respond:

I go from home to bridge and from bridge to home. I enter the secret room and drink until I'm fed up of the blood of our lord. But today... today Jesus bleeds green, chlorophyll green- That's how Teofila bled.

The toad imitates a prostitute saying:

-I think about eating and the damn toad obsessively —comments the white viceroy before becoming a crow and cawing to the moon-.

I have decided to become vegetarian, I shall only eat pumpkins and tomatoes, once in a while, I shall light the joint.

This cannibal toad seems more primitive than the orthodox image that the white viceroy keeps in his mind, to know: pot full of white cooking adventures between carrots and other vegetables. The cooked –Levi Strauss would say- is a sign of major evolution. Then were does a teethed toad belong to?

-Well, isn't this the present? –The toad jumps and falls on the left shoulder of the white viceroy-. Belong to an era of the raw, I hate overcooked steaks that other middle class members devour, feeling vanguard of present civilization.

-What's the difference between beak and mouth? –asked, wanting to change the conversation-. What difference is there between branch and arm? Between green consciousness and Christian consciousness?

-What's the difference between horror narration and HEMOFICTION? –Inquires the white viceroy, introducing the toad in his hat. The animal disappears a few seconds but comes out again, leaping, from the viceroys dressed in black hat.

-HEMOFICTION analyzes and dialogues –explains the viceroy dressed in black, doing faces and gestures just like his contrary-. It's about a natural tendency of enchantment by blood –irrational inclination, poetic and disgusting-, combined with mentioned incidents with the necessity to decipher the unpractical labyrinths programmed in destructive and murderous minds. Minds possessed by the demon of the green, plants grow in the brain and man returns to his progenitors state and it later becomes another plant, stem. Then, in reality, the identity of the plant shall struggle in ourselves through the drug.

-The secret identity of my person comes close to the green, back to the abysm of roots thanks to alcohol, thanks to weed and to cocaine.

-I felt love and ate my frog. I was hungry and started to eat my little toad –assured the toad in a sorry tone, kissing the neck of the viceroy dressed in white, who makes a face of disgust and hits the toad so it falls on his feet again.

-You see, at times I feel instead of blood in my veins runs milk. I am dizzy with red. I'm afraid if I am squeezed I shall squirt green chlorophyll.

I thought of red milk while I chewed on my frog and my little toad –croaked the toad, kissing the right ankle of the white viceroy.

-HEMOFICTION fascinates before dogmas, clichés, prejudice, crimes, vices, illnesses –the black viceroy has lighted a cigarette that releases dark smoke, opposite color of the smoke that his twin expels. The toad also smokes and throws a gray colored smoke, which smells like vanilla.

-Yellow perversity, the men –most- deep inside are good –comments the white viceroy, putting on his black hat of the viceroy dressed in black at the same time he shakes off the toad who leaps in the air-. The age of the raw has gone.

It is not the moment to paint the body nor carry bones in the nose.

My voracious appetites have finished during the joining. The couples touch each other keeping exquisite sweetness in mind.

-I hug my girlfriend without hunger –the viceroy dressed in white caws.

-But your girlfriend who knows –replies the toad.

The three characters project to a time when their cigarettes didn't do a thing.

-Horror for the horror- states the white viceroy, hitting Anselmo's back who still doesn't wake up. Congestion. The floral complot has, deeply, corroded everything.

-I wish to become a flower, grow in a pot and be placed in the hallway of a house, any house, even in one with only four walls.

-I don't interrogate, close, but fat nightmares do filter through cracks on the door –the viceroy dressed in white kicks the toad lightly, who wants to pose once again on the right foot, but the toad immediately goes back and cuddles onto the left foot, the sinister-. The unconsciousness is the evil. The toad is the evil. Ideal agent to the flowers.

The gray toad croaks on the left foot of the milky viceroy:

-I felt satisfaction after devouring my lover and little toad. So much that I felt like having my legitimate wife for lunch –jumping inside the hat and immediately shouting out loud: *Get me out of here.*

-The road to the unreachable shimmer gives sense to the works of Hemofiction –indicates the viceroy dressed in black, smelling the interior of the hat where black hands submerges and frees the toad. He deposits it on the floor and the toad eructs and turns into a mouse. Eructs and turns into a cricket. Eructs and into a spider. Eructs and into a geranium. Milky viceroy hits the bug, which intends to climb his leg, squashes it with the sole and stares at it with fear and disgust. We have taken out the evil and chaos is ordered. The evil from the green world is coming. Chlorophyll.

-The witches in real life didn't exist- the black viceroy clarifies-. Church invented them to keep the belongings of naïve rich.

Once again the toad out of the black hat croaks and jumper to the feet of the viceroy dressed in white. Eructs and turns into a cat. Eructs and is a chicken. Eructs and becomes a toad again, but with a lettuce as a head. It was no good that our milky plan should squash him, it comes out of the hat over and over again.

-I renounce to look inside of the hat of insanity again –affirms the white viceroy, throwing faraway the black hat same that returns flying in the hands of his equal.

The viceroy dressed in black says:

-The mother of Jack the Ripper could have been my perfect house wife, just like the one of Count Dracula. I am capable of imagining them in the kitchen preparing pussy, while their children slurp blood or pull out guts.

-Evil always boils close to kitchens, jails or caverns. There is no doubt that it is related to tables. I caw flying to the wardrobe-. There's no doubt that the vegetables have invaded my consciousness. I stay away from the crimes of Teofila.

The toad croaks leaping from shoe to shoe:

-I have swum in the blood that springs from a deep stab wound.

-Then, what is Hemofictión? –asks the white viceroy.

-Strinberg said that during his life he tried to find God and only found the devil. The same way Hemofiction finds consciousness, but it always finds itself in the unconsciousness –I comment from my place at the wardrobe, looking with horror that four-bugambilia branches have gotten through into the room.

-Christian dreams- the toads blurs out, jumping to the right foot of the white viceroy.

-Not Christian, blasphemy -the viceroy dressed in white points out putting the toad back into the black hat.

-Christian consciousness –insists the toad before submerging in the puddle of the magical hat.

-Satan exists. He has rose red eyes and black lips like orchids.

-Man chooses whether to make a pact with the devil, but sometimes the demonic election is imposed from the inside, as if the individual was possessed, as if in another existence and cape of consciousness the pact was done without showing off or memory.

-Christian consciousness, confess in front of the devil's pot —asks the toad.

-Christian consciousness on top of the church and sects, on top of Christ himself, when he is used in bellicose and torturous conceptions.

-Of course. That is why Christ chose the Christians who put him in judgment cloth —croaks the toad jumping out of the hat.

-Of course not – remarks the milky viceroy moving to avoid the toad falling on him again.

-Maybe the pot of the non-existing witches is full of Christmas punch —the toad croaks on the right foot of the viceroy dressed in white-. Inside boils Teofila's corpse.

-I don't drink. I am a viceroy of good —states the viceroy dressed in white.

-And I am, too —responds the toad-, but I drink until I turn myself into a hallucination.

-HEMOFICTION underlines the instinct possession –the white viceroy points out, trying to avoid that the toad continues to jump from shoe to shoe. It continuous jumps produced the milky viceroy sensations of doubt as to vice and evilness, with respect to space and time-. The toad jumps and the world turns, and the sun turns, and the cosmos moves in an awful way to the rhythm of a damned boiling inside the dark hat.

-To more consciousness more reality. Another reality that opposed realism (immediate situation that dominated the sense of view.

-What I see is –states the milky.

-I see what is not- the black.

-I see what is and what not is –the toad.

-I don't see what is not –whitey.

-Ideal toad, the white viceroy denies to see me.

-Stories must be told what happens outside and ignores the intestines where the toad lives –suggests the viceroy dressed in white-. For me, let's put out the cauldron, it has boiled too much. The disgusting toad disappears.

-Reality, which adopts a psyche with a possibility of simultaneous in existence and/or dual personalities – the black viceroy has gone to convert into a crow and peck Anselmo's face, almost turned into jacaranda. Suddenly the servant opens its mouth and snores all it can, crazy train. And suddenly -horror- it stops making noise. And makes a deep silence. Little blue jacaranda flowers grow covering its eyes, nose and mouth.

-Legend form, half true history and half fantasy –eructs the toad and becomes a mouse. Eructs and cricket.

-I like lineal narrations –comments whitey.

-The HEMOFICTIVE narration is expansive and non-lineal –says the toad, jumping to the interior of the black hat and cauldron at the same time.

-It's the consciousness of God that must guide a hero –declares the viceroy dressed in white-. Evil suppresses in pages left in white.

Anselmo and I have fallen into the vortex of dream. Both of us are descending –proliferating branches, leaves, seeds and roots –until finding a great mouth made of leaves and flowers. Effective drug conduces the return to contemplate in front of Green-God. Tomorrow I shall be stem and crow, not person and animal anymore.

Glossary

Agave: Blue Maguey, a plant from which tequila is extracted.

Bugambilia: Purple and red flower that grows in the Mexican tropics.

Cuba / Cuba Libre: Drink made out of coca cola and rum.

Fabada: Spanish stew.

Llorona: Mexican legend of a crying woman.

Pulquerias: Places where Pulque, Mexican alcoholic drink, is sold.

Talavera: Place where ceramic is made.

Tamalera: Woman who sells tamales.

About the Author

Juan Trigos (1941-)

Creator of the aesthetic literary style Hemofiction. Literature of search which reflects on the bleeding of the consciousness in multiple mirrors, where it contemplates with horror the thousand faces of personal infantilism, process which endures desolation and anguish, indispensable symptoms on the road to individuation, path of ascension towards human. To be, it is necessary to suffer an internal revolution, practically impossible to reach. Maybe, someday, the spiritual awakening leads man to paradise –another dimension of consciousness- which could mean the full responsibility of which most characters, created by Juan Trigos, run away from, precisely by humans. Hemofiction opens doors to the personal conscience of the author and, through expansive reflection, towards the intimate knowledge of the adult reader, who is capable to glimpse into ones own abysms. He stands against the europeanized concept of literature history, all class of paradigms that oblige copy and diminished positions in writers that start from a different spine for their creations and, for the same, do not belong, nor want to belong, to a universal abstract cultural sphere which tends to simplify the extreme richness of the soul. Hemofiction is serious literature, points towards the exit of the everyday insane asylum. Invents realities which seem like games where the spiritual depth is illuminated by experience. This extraordinary writer looks with pitiless objectivity the most darkest tendencies of the human being. The works which have given him fame, are all now united under the seal of Fontamara: Cuento del Perro Bailarín, Déjame que te mate para ver si te extraño, La Llorona, Mulata del Diablo, La Leyenda de Don Juan Manuel, La Diabólica Santa de las Tijeras, Callejón de las Ratas, Policías y Rateros, El Maniático Hombre de la Bacinica, Leyenda del Sapo Matón, Crímenes en la Profesa, Rincón de las Calaveras, Leyenda del Hombre Verde, Diario de un Cuervo Humano, Mamá es loca o está poseída, El Tapado, Castigo,

Divino Placer, La Guillotinita, La Culpa, JuanCamaleón, el hombre mimético, Carne y Tripas de Gusano, Hijo de Tamalera, Confesión de una Muerta, Nuestra Señora del Rostro Rasurado, Araña Negra y Peluda, La Zarpa, Cuentos de Hemoficción, Leyenda de los Espíritus, Yo digo que soy yo, pero quién sabe, El Hombre-Reloj; and now in English: La Llorona, Let me kill you to see if I miss you, The Guilt and Diary of a Human Crow.

www.ingramcontent.com/pod-product-compliance
Lightning Source LLC
Chambersburg PA
CBHW020420290526
45785CB00002B/644